THE WHEEL OF TIME
The Kalachakra In Context

THE WHEEL OF TIME
The Kalachakra In Context

Geshe Lhundub Sopa
Roger Jackson
John Newman

With a Foreword by
His Holiness the Dalai Lama

Edited by Beth Simon

Snow Lion Publications
Ithaca, New York, USA

Snow Lion Publications
P.O. Box 6483
Ithaca, New York 14851
USA

Copyright © 1985 Deer Park
First published by Deer Park Books, Madison, 1985.
First Snow Lion Publications edition, 1991.

Printed in the USA

ISBN 1-55939-001-8

Contents

Preface

Initiation into the complex and profound Kalachakra ("Wheel of Time") tantra has been granted with increasing frequency in recent years, both in Asia and in the West, most often by H. H. the Fourteenth Dalai Lama. This, in turn, has led to a growing interest in the Kalachakra on the part of Buddhist practitioners, scholars and the public. However, this growing interest has not been reflected in a significant increase in available information on the Kalachakra; that remains sparse. This book is intended, in its modest way, to help enlarge our picture of this most important Buddhist meditational tradition.

We would like to clarify at the outset what this book is, and is not. It is not an exploration of the subtleties and arcana of the astrology (an important part of the Outer Kalachakra) or the subtle physiology (of the Inner Kalachakra) of the Kalachakra system. These are terribly complex and little understood topics, and we could not hope to do them justice here. Nor is this a practitioner's manual, for it contains no actual rituals or sadhanas. These, we feel, ought to be available at the discretion of the initiating lama to those with proper initiation. Therefore, we felt these were best left out of a book such as this, whose circulation may be more general.

What the book does provide, we hope, is a relatively clear overview of the history and yoga of the Kalachakra system. We have attempted to place the Kalachakra within the context of Buddhism as a whole, to present something of the history of the Kalachakra, and then to outline the procedures involved in each of the three major aspects of Kalachakra yoga: initiation, sadhana, and the six-limbed yoga of the completion stage. These three topics are what is covered in the last three of the five chapters of the *Kalachakra Tantra*, concerning the Other Kalachakra, that is, the purification of the Outer and the Inner Kalachakras presented in the first two chapters.

We have striven for a balance between excessively detailed scholarship, which often can obscure the general picture, and over-generalization, which often does violence to the nuances of context. Our hope is that, at the very least, the reader may emerge with a clearer sense of the place of the Kalachakra system in the Buddhist meditational tradition, of the history of the Kalachakra, and of the structures involved in its practice.

The articles collected here were written at different times for different purposes. The first and fourth articles were written as part of an earlier planned Kalachakra book project that has evolved into the present volume. The second article was written especially for this work. The third article was prepared as a paper for delivery at the sixth conference of the International Association of Buddhist Studies, 1983. The fifth article was published as "An Excursus on the Subtle Body in Tantric Buddhism" in vol. 6, no. 2, 1982, of *The Journal of the International Association of Buddhist Studies*. (We wish to thank the *Journal* for permission to reprint the article.)

We should like to Edward Bastian and Tenzin Trinley for their work and suggestions early in the project. Elvin Jones and David Patt, of the Deer Park Editorial Advisory Board, provided both concrete and moral support throughout the project.

Several people helped with word processing and proofreading: Anna Allred, Mary Bingham, Nancy Douglas, Kathy Downs, Jan Conrad, Cathy Kennedy, and Jane Sillman. Maurice Thaler gave needed, professional assistance with computer use and ix

photography. Marlene Gisser, as Art Director, oversaw book and cover design and production. Steve Deatherage made many excellent suggestions regarding typography, and worked some very long nights as well. Beth Simon, as Copy Editor, standardized translations and transliterations, gave stylistic cohesion to the book, and generally saw the project through the final stages.

Our deepest debt of gratitude is owed to H. H. the Fourteenth Dalai Lama, who granted the Kalachakra initiation at Deer Park in Madison, Wisconsin, US, in July, 1981, and who encouraged this project from its inception. Our gratitude is owed, as well, to the late Khyabje Serkhong Rinpoche, who gave preparatory teachings on the Kalachakra at Deer Park, 1980, and then returned to give the rare instruction of the sadhana-practice in July, 1982. Much of what is contained in this book is a direct or indirect reflection of the compassionate wisdom of these two, and it is to the long life of H. H. the Dalai Lama, and to the quick return of Khyabje Serkhong Rinpoche that we dedicate this work.

Geshe Lhundub Sopa
Roger Jackson
John Newman

Foreword
Concerning the Kalachakra

The notion and sense of "I" is a mere projection on the four or five psychophysical aggregates which make up the person. Yet this sense of "I" which we all possess, even the smallest insect, innately seeks to find satisfaction and to avoid misery.

In order to establish desirable states of happiness and to eliminate undesirable states of frustration and sorrow, the various kinds of living beings apply themselves according to their individual capacities to the activities that will achieve these goals. The happiness to be produced and the sorrows to be eliminated are of many types. A human being, for example, gains a type of happiness from food, shelter and social success. This person experiences much suffering when these are taken away, but if one were to ask whether the limits of joy and sorrow end here, the answer is negative. No matter how much food, shelter and social success one has, these external conditions alone will not produce a lasting happiness if one's mind is disturbed by spiritual uneasiness. This indicates that, in addition to concerning ourselves with physical and environmental well-being, we must try to create a basis of inner peace and spiritual well-being.

Which happiness is stronger, that arising from external conditions or that from spiritual well-being? If one has the latter, then circumstances for suffering do not arise even when the external conditions of happiness fail to converge. Alternatively, when one is bereft of inner peace, the most pleasant external situation is unable to bring happiness into the mind. In this sense, the inner state of the mind is much more important than the state of external conditions. Therefore, it is essential that we ourselves know the means by which a state of inner peace is created and cultivated. This would benefit us individually in a very immediate, practical and down-to-earth sense. Furthermore, in this era when there is so much social tension on the earth, when the nations of the world are themselves so intensely concerned with competition and efforts to overpower one another, even at the threat of nuclear devastation, it is most urgent for us to try to develop spiritual wisdom.

At present, the world is not lacking in technological or industrial development. What we are lacking is a basis for mental or spiritual harmony and joy. Were we to cultivate the gentle pleasures of a loving and compassionate mind, for example, we would personally experience peace, even when confronted by external turmoil, and we would have a pacifying effect on our chaotic environment. If, on the other hand, our mind is controlled by such qualities as greed, jealousy, aggression, pride and so forth, instead of by spiritual qualities, then even the most attractive external conditions will bring very little comfort to the mind. Therefore, this inner peace and joy not only benefits the individual who develops it; it also benefits the entire human community.

What does Buddhism have to contribute to the human quest for spiritual well-being? The root of the Buddhadharma is the teaching of the Four Noble Truths seen by the Sublime Ones. The Four Noble Truths are suffering, its causes, liberation from suffering, and the path to such liberation. The truth of suffering refers to the various levels of misery, frustration and pain that we must learn to recognize. We usually mistake the subtle forms of suffering for excitement and pleasure. When we identify suffering as suffering, the mind takes on an aversion to it. Therefore, after speaking of suffering, the Buddha taught its source or cause.

First of all, do the undesirable states of suffering that we experience arise from causes or do they arise without cause? Second, if their causes can be identified, can they also be eliminated? These are important questions. When one perceives that in fact there are various ways to eliminate all causes of misery, one arrives at a certain conviction in one's own spiritual abilities. From this is born a mind that will work for liberation.

Therefore, the Buddha taught the Third Noble Truth, the truth of cessation, or the liberation from suffering. When one sees that a state of spiritual well-being totally beyond suffering can be generated, one understands that liberation is something that must be achieved within the mind itself, not through any other object. When the stains and aberrations of one's own mind have been purified in the mind's final nature, liberation is achieved. This being so, we should cultivate the liberating techniques within our own mindstream and eradicate all such distorting factors and obscurations as attachment and the other delusions that so strongly influence our present way of being. We must reverse deluded habits of thought born from misunderstanding reality, and actualize a perfectly pure mind.

Here "perfectly pure mind" refers to the consciousness that has totally eradicated the mental habits of incorrectly apprehending objects of knowledge. To accomplish this, one must generate an awareness of emptiness, or the way things actually exist. When this awareness arises, the mind that mistakenly apprehends its objects can be put to rest. We should use our ability to destroy from within ourselves the confused habits of thought of wrongly perceiving things, of seeing them other than the way they exist, by generating this awareness of the ultimate mode of existence of reality. The Buddha taught that by generating this awareness of the ultimate mode, and then meditating on it single-pointedly, all mental distortion is eliminated.

This ultimate mode of things has been explained by various means in order to suit the individual capacity and needs of various kinds of disciples. The Buddha taught four major schools of thought to his followers to provide them with a path which they could begin by practicing first on the lower views of reality as a means of preparing themselves for the higher. When put to the test of reason, some of these schools withstand analysis and some exhibit logical faults. Similarly, we must critically examine all the teachings and discern those which are literally true, and those which are lower doctrines given by the Buddha in accordance with a specific time and need, and therefore require interpretation. Those teachings which, when tested, reveal logical flaws must be approached accordingly.

Of the four schools of thought, the *Madhyamaka* School presents the most accurate description of the ultimate truth. We should therefore try to understand its teachings on the ultimate nature of reality by carefully studying and meditating on its authoritative scriptures.

In order to be able to generate inner spiritual forces which are able to destroy the various mental distortions, one must engage a powerful method. The more powerful the method, the stronger becomes one's application to the view of emptiness. When one's method is strong, one's meditations on emptiness become very powerful and one's ability to destroy negative habits of thought are intensified.

On the basis of the vastness of the methods used, the Buddha's teachings are divided into two main vehicles: the Bodhisattva Vehicle and the Shravaka Vehicle, generally known as the Mahayana and the Hinayana respectively.

In the method of the Bodhisattva Vehicle, one meditates that everything one does is for the benefit of living beings. Once it has been understood that all living beings, just like oneself, want happiness and dislike suffering, the attitude assuming responsibility for their well-being arises. This attitude is an amazing, wonderful and most courageous force, more precious than anything else in existence. When used as a basis for one's meditation upon the ultimate mode of things, the forces that destroy delusion and distortion are easily cultivated.

What are the methods of meditating on this altruistic mind-to-enlightenment in conjunction with meditation on emptiness as explained in the great *Madhyamaka* works?

These methods are classified in accordance with the "coarseness" or "subtlety" of the level of consciousness performing the meditation. Factors such as the subtlety and the force and nature of one's mind strongly influence one's experience of the view of emptiness.

How so? The coarse levels of consciousness will not produce an experience of emptiness as quickly as will the subtle. Whether the coarse or subtle mind engaged in meditation is doing so on the basis of a union of method and wisdom also affects the nature of the practice. A meditation in which method and wisdom are not kept in union will not produce tremendous results. When the mind is absorbed in method and wisdom conjoined, meditation on emptiness is most effective.

According to the schools of Buddhist thought that accept six spheres of consciousness, that is, the five sensory consciousnesses together with purely mental consciousness, there is both a coarse or ordinary level of consciousness that can perform meditation on emptiness on the basis of method and wisdom combined, and a subtle level of consciousness able to perform this meditation. Once one has cultivated a subtle level of consciousness propelled by the vast mind-to-enlightenment and applied it to realization of emptiness, the meditation becomes extremely powerful and is able to destroy quickly the host of destructive mental traits.

Where can be found the practices of the coarse level of consciousness which counteracts delusion by means of undivided method and wisdom? According to the *Sambhuta Tantra*, there are four classes of tantras: *Kriya, Charya,* Yoga and *Anuttara* Yoga tantras In the three lower tantras, one generates a coarse consciousness combining method and wisdom, and then meditates on emptiness. The yogic techniques for engaging the powerful, subtle levels of consciousness focused in meditation born from the inseparability of method and wisdom are found only in the texts of *Anuttara* or highest Yoga tantra.

To generate this subtle level of consciousness, one must first eliminate the agitation of the coarse level of conceptual thought. Many methods for effecting this end have been taught. One such method found in the highest yoga tantra involves arresting the deceptive projections of conceptual thought by means of channeling the vital energies of the nervous system. In a second method one cuts off the movements of conceptual thought and engages in totally non-conceptual meditation in order to eliminate the elements that distort the mind.

A number of different approaches to this yogic path have been expounded. Here I will speak briefly about the meditative techniques found in the Kalachakra tantra. This tantra belongs to the class of highest yoga tantras.

What constitutes the path of the Kalachakra tantra?

Kalachakra is a tantric system with several unique characteristics. Generally, *Anuttara* tantra systems are of two types: hidden tantras, such as the Guhyasamaja, and clear tantras, such as the Kalachakra. The difference between these two systems appears in the fourth initiation. In the hidden tantras, the fourth initiation is revealed in a very concealed manner, whereas in the clear tantras, it is presented very clearly.

Although basically all the individual systems found in the highest yoga tantra are equally profound, they each have their own approach which renders them more effective as a practice in accordance with the specific nature of the individual practitioner's vital energies, nervous system, psychic predispositions, karmic tendencies, and so forth. If one practices the highest yoga tantra system most appropriate to one's personal situation, the effect will be far more powerful than meditating on any other system of the same class of tantra.

It is important that the practitioner engages in the system most suited to him or her. To demonstrate this metaphorically, a sick person takes a medicine appropriate to the specific illness and to the general condition of the person's being. All systems in the highest yoga tantras are equally powerful, but a difference between them appears in their application to the physical, psychic and karmic situation of the individual practitioner. This is obvious from the different ways in which people experience the manifestations of the subtle consciousness and energies such as in the visions of smoke and so forth at the time of death.

The Kalachakra tantra is a very special tantra for those who have the correct body, mind and karmic predispositions. These special qualities become apparent after one has completed the imagined creation stage yogas and engages in the unfeigned completion stage practices. The Kalachakra tantra is unique in its presentation of the six yogas that constitute its completion stage. It is not appropriate to discuss these topics openly.

As for the meditation of the Kalachakra tantra's creation stage that ripens and matures the mind for the completion stage yogas, three Kalachakras are taught. Outer, or External, Kalachakra constitutes the elements of the universe in which we live; Inner, or Internal, Kalachakra constitutes the psychophysical aggregates, sensory and psychic capacities of the living being; Other, or Alter-Kalachakra is the path of the creation and completion stage yogas that have the power to purify the above two Kalachakras.

Outer Kalachakra is generally explained in the context of this planet Earth. When one meditates on the mandala of Kalachakra, Inner Kalachakra is seen as the body, faces, hands, feet, etc., as well as all the surrounding deities of the mandala, conceived as symbols of the stars, planets, constellations, and so forth. From this we can understand that Kalachakra has a special connection with all the people of this planet.

From the point of view of the personage at whose request the Kalachakra tantra was expounded, unlike any other tantra, Kalachakra was taught at the request of Chandrabhadra, King of the legendary Shambhala, who, for the benefit of the subjects of the ninety-six kingdoms of his land, travelled to India and requested such a teaching from the Buddha. Kalachakra therefore has a special relationship with one particular land on this earth. From Chandrabhadra, the lineage has been passed down through a line of seven Great Kings and twenty-one Kulika Kings, beginning with Manjushrikirti. In the coming of the twenty-fifth Kulika King, the special connection that the people of this earth share with Kalachakra will be strongly manifested in world events.

In general, the Kalachakra tantra, like any highest yoga tantra, is meant for practitioners of the highest faculty. Nonetheless, due to the above considerations, it was the tradition in Tibet to give openly the Kalachakra initiation.

Although Shambhala is a place located somewhere on this planet, it is a place that can be seen only by those whose minds and karmic propensities are pure. The Buddha taught in accordance with the predispositions of destiny existing within the practitioners. For the average person, he taught the paths of the Shravaka Vehicle and the Pratyekabuddha Vehicle. To the practitioners of a purer karmic predisposition, he taught the Bodhisattva Vehicle, that is, the common Mahayana or Great Vehicle. For the few of highest faculties, he appeared in various forms, sometimes as a monk and sometimes as a tantric deity, and taught the three lower of the four classes of tantras. In the form of deities embodying the inseparable union of method and wisdom, he taught the highest yoga tantra.

xviii

Because these teachings were given in mystical manifestations
of the Buddha to those in a mystical state of purified karma and
perception, it does not matter much whether any specific tantra in
question was expounded during the life of the historical Buddha.
Yet, in fact, the *Root Tantra (Mula Tantra)* of Kalachakra was set forth
by the Buddha during his life. The Buddha's direct disciple, King
Chandrabhadra, composed the first *Commentary to the Root Tantra
(Kalachakra Tantra Tika)*, and Manjushrikirti, the first Kulika King,
composed a *Condensed Tantra (Laghu Kalachakra)*. Manjushrikirti's
son, Pundarika, then composed a great commentary entitled *Stainless Light (Vimalaprabha)*. Thus the Kalachakra tantra was spread
widely throughout Shambhala.

Eventually Chilupa (circa 10th century, AD), a master from eastern India, traveled to Shambhala in search of the Kalachakra tantra. On the way he met an incarnation of the Bodhisattva Manjushri, and received from him the initiation, scriptures,
commentaries and oral transmissions of Kalachakra. Chilupa eventually passed the lineage to the Bengali-born pandit Acharya. From
him it passed to such masters as Kalachakrapada the First, Kalachakrapada the Second, the Nalanda sage Manjukirti, and the
Tibetan monk Sang Gye Yeshe, who had come from Khams Prov-
ince of Tibet, worked his way up the hierarchy of Bodh Gaya
Monastery and become its abbot; and to the Nepali pandit
Samanta Shribhadra. Thus it gradually spread through India and
Nepal.

The Tibetan yogi Ra Chorab (12th century, A.D.), traveled to
Nepal to study Kalachakra under Samanta Shribhadra, and eventually invited this teacher to Tibet. There they translated into Tibetan
all the main scriptures related to Kalachakra. Ra Chorab passed the
lineage to his principal disciple, Ra Yeshe Seng Gye, and eventually
it came to Bu ston Rin chen Drub (14th century, A.D.). Thus the
lineage has been passed from generation to generation until the
present day. I, myself, received the initiations and the transmissions
of teachings on the creation and completion stages from my Vajra
Teacher Kyabje Ling Dorje Chang, the Ninety-seventh Patriarch to
Tsong kha pa's Throne. I received the transmission of the *Commentary to the Root Tantra* from Serkhong Tukse Rinpoche.

The higher meditations of the Kalachakra tantra can be practised only by a select few; but because of past and future events, and

in order to establish a strong karmic relationship with Kalachakra in the minds of the people, there is now a tradition of giving the initiation to large public gatherings.

The following are qualifications of someone who wishes to receive the Kalachakra transmission for actual practice. In terms of the level of *bodhicitta* or the mind-to-enlightenment that cherishes others more than oneself: the best disciple dwells in an unfeigned experience of this sublime mind; the medium disciple has had a small flash of it in meditations; the lowest should have at least an intense appreciation for and interest in developing it. In terms of the philosophical development: the best disciple has an undistorted experience of the nature of ultimate reality as explained in either the *Madhyamaka* or *Yogachara* schools of Mahayana thought; the medium disciple has a correct understanding based on study and reason; the lowest disciple should have at least a strong appreciation for and interest in learning the philosophical views of either of the two above-mentioned schools. In addition, a disciple seeking the Kalachakra initiation should have faith and interest in this particular system. The purpose of initiation is to plant certain karmic seeds in the mind of the recipient; if he or she does not possess the openness of a certain degree of spiritual interest, it will be very difficult for the seeds to take hold.

If one wishes to receive the initiation merely as a blessing, that is, in order to establish a karmic relationship with the Kalachakra tantra, initiation on this basis can be given to anyone who sincerely appreciates the opportunity. Even if in one's faith one does not comprehend the principles of the path combining method and wisdom as explained above, the seed of initiation can be placed in one's mind if one has the smallest basis of faith. Therefore this is the minimum qualification required to attend such an initiation.

As explained above, at the moment, our minds are bound by impure habits of thought. We must dissolve these impure modes of perception and distorted patterns of thought into the dharmadhatu reality. Should we accomplish this, the purposes of Buddhadharma, of the Mahayana, of the Vajrayana, of highest yoga tantra, of the Kalachakra tantra and of having received the Kalachakra initiation will have been fulfilled. Though this is difficult, the effort is well worthwhile, and we should energetically apply ourselves to it.

His Holiness the 14th Dalai Lama

THE WHEEL OF TIME

Kalachakra In Context

ROGER JACKSON

SHAKYAMUNI AND KALACHAKRA: WESTERN AND TRADITIONAL VIEWS

Buddhism is a vast and diverse religious tradition, but whether the image of the Buddha that we conjure is a delicate sandstone carving from Sarnath, the great bronze statue at Kamakura, or a weather-worn volcanic rock sculpture from Borobudur, the features are likely to be the same: the meditation posture, the finely draped robes, the crown protuberance, the separately curled hairs, the pendant earlobes, the eyes neither quite open nor quite closed, and, above all, the smile—that elusive half-smile that suggests at once personal satisfaction in the transcendance of worldly suffering and compassion for beings still mired in the round of unwanted rebirths that is cyclic existence.

This is the Buddha best known, but it is not the Buddha's only form. The Mahayana tradition, which has shaped Buddhism in China, Japan, Korea, Tibet, Mongolia, and Vietnam, allows that the Buddha, both during this lifetime and after the death of his physical body, appeared in a multitude of forms, some human and some non-human, some visible to ordinary beings ande some visible only

to the spiritually advanced, some benign and some wrathful. To
many Tibetan Buddhists, the Buddha's supreme emanation, the
form in which he taught his most profound and most comprehen-
sive doctrines and practices, was as Kalachakra, the personification
of the "Wheel of Time."

How different from the Buddha of Sarnath, Kamakura, or
Borobudur does this tantric deity appear! In Tibetan painted scroll
images, he stands in the center of a lotus blossom in sexual union
with a consort. He has four faces and twenty-four arms, in various
colors, each of which holds a weapon or ritual implement. Be-
decked by jewels, wearing only loose silks, and a tiger skin, he and
his consort crush demons underfoot. His long hair is piled up in
the manner of a yogi. His eyes—of which each face has three—are
wide open, and his teeth are bared.

What possible connection can this complex, perhaps frighten-
ing figure have with the serene Buddhas with which we are so
familiar? What possible relation is there between the menacing
grin of Kalachakra and the gentle smile of Shakyamuni? The
attempt to answer these questions takes one to the heart of the
differences between the Western scholarly and Buddhist traditional ways of viewing the history of Buddhism, and particularly
the place of the tantric tradition within that history.

Most contemporary Western-trained scholars view the history
of religion diachronically, as a process of constant development in
the face of internal and external challenges, often unforseen by the
religion's founder. Many contemporary scholars tend to be distrust-
ful of traditionalist accounts of the development of a particular
religion, and to rely heavily on critical textual analysis in settling
problems of dating, authenticity, etc. Thus, a typical contemporary
historian of Buddhism would concede that a religious teacher who
styled himself "the Buddha," (the enlightened one,) probably did
live sometime in the sixth or fifth century B.C., but that historian
would quickly add that the oldest Buddhist texts were compiled
more than two centuries after the Buddha's death, so we cannot be
certain exactly what he taught or in what form. It is more than
likely that the Pali canon, despite its claims of genuine antiquity, is
an admixture of authentic fragments and later interpolations.

The Mahayana, whose earliest scriptures cannot be dated
before the first century B.C., probably was not taught by the

Buddha himself. Rather, it represents a development out of schisms among earlier Buddhist sects. It also represents a reaction to philosophical and religious changes outside the Buddhist fold, such as the rise of Hindu bhakti devotionalism.

Therefore, if, as many contemporary scholars believe, Mahayana sutras probably were not spoken by the Buddha, then it is even less likely that he spoke the tantras attributed to him. Tantrism, despite an ancestry that may be pre-Vedic and indigenous to the Indian subcontinent, was articulated rather late in the course of Indian religious history. It probably began as an unorthodox, doctrinally ambiguous, and magically-oriented movement that gradually was absorbed by and adapted to the more established religious traditions, Buddhism among them.

The Buddhist tantra generally conceded to be the earliest, the Guhyasamaja, dates from the fourth century A.D. at the earliest, while the Kalachakra tantra is among the latest, appearing in India no earlier than the ninth or tenth century. Thus, in the view of many contemporary scholars, tantra has virtually nothing to do with what the Buddha actually may have taught, for it is the product of a different age with different religious needs and circumstances. Thus, the problem of the relation between Shakymuni and Kalachakra might be explained by the assertion that Shakyamuni did not teach the *Kalachakra Tantra*, although it represents one possible form of his teaching after nearly 1500 years of evolution.

Buddhist tradition tends to view the teaching to the Dharma synchronically, as a complete and self-contained explanation of the cosmos, taught one way or the other by the Buddha during his historical tenure on earth. All Buddhist traditions will concede that the Buddha's teachings have required elucidation by subsequent commentators, but each tradition will steadfastly maintain that the words it attributes to the Buddha actually were spoken by him. Theravadin tradition, therefore, holds that the *suttas* contained in the Pali canon are exactly as spoken by the Buddha. At the same time, Theravadins reject as spurious the sutras and tantras attributed to the Buddha by Mahayanists. Mahayanists in Tibet, China, and other Asian countries generally accept as the authentic word of the Buddha any sutra or tantra attributed to him and translated into their language from an Indian language. They assert that during his 45-year teaching career the Buddha expounded the "Hinayana" sutras accepted by Theravadins, such Mahayana sutras as the *Lotus, Lankavatara,* and the Perfection of Wisdom series, and such tantras as the *Guhyasamaja, Chakrasamvara, Hevajra*—and the *Kalachakra.*

Mahayanists concede that the Mahayana sutras generally came to prominence in Indian Buddhism later than the Hinayana sutras, and the tantras later still, but attribute this to the occasional removal of a sutra or tradition from the cultural mainstream. Thus, the Perfection of Wisdom sutras are said to have been hidden under the ocean by creatures called nagas until they were brought back to India by Nagarjuna. The tantric practices of Kalachakra are said to have been preserved and transmitted for centuries in the land of Shambala, until restored to India by Chilupa in the ninth or tenth century.

Thus, for a Mahayana Buddhist—particularly for a Tibetan Buddhist—there is neither a historical nor a spiritual discrepancy between Shakyamuni and Kalachakra, for each was a form in which the Buddha manifested and taught, and the teachings of each are consonant and resonant with the teachings of the other.

For many contemporary scholars, then, the serene smile of Shakyamuni and the terrifying smile of Kalachakra are centuries apart in time, and worlds apart in significance. For a Tibetan Buddhist, they coincide: they are the smiles of the same being, and reflect the same vision of the universe and the same ultimate spiritual attainment. They are both manifestations of the Buddha, differing, to the degree that they do, only because the needs and abilities of beings who strive for liberation differ.

The traditional and the contemporary scholarly versions of the history of Buddhism are profoundly, perhaps irrevocably opposed, based as they are on radically differing views not only on how evidence is to be weighed in the determination of religious history, but also on the place and potential of the mind within the scheme of the cosmos.

We will not enter here into a discussion of the relative merits of the two approaches—each has its own strengths and weaknesses— for we are concerned in this chapter not with historical argument (a risky undertaking at best) but with placing the Kalachakra tantra within the context of the living Tibetan Buddhist tradition of which it is a part. Perforce, then, we will describe the Kalachakra as it is seen by a Tibetan Buddhist traditionalist: in synchronic and organic relation to the rest of the Buddha's teachings. From within Tibetan Buddhism, we will adopt the viewpoint of the *dGe lug pa* school, the tradition that gave rise to the institution of Dalai Lamas, and to which belong the masters responsible for transmitting and teaching the Kalachakra system to the present Dalai Lama—who in turn now has transmitted and taught the Kalachakra in India, America and Europe.

THE LIFE OF THE BUDDHA

Any account of Buddhism must begin with the life of its founder and continuing inspiration, Shakyamuni Buddha, who was born Siddhartha Gautama in the small north Indian state of Shakya around 560 B.C., renounced the world at 29, was enlightened under a pipal tree near Gaya at 35, and taught his Dharma for 45 years until his death at Kushinagara around 480 B.C. Most Buddhist traditions are in general agreement on the events of the Buddha's life. The Mahayana tradition usually divides his life into twelve major acts:

1. Seeing that the time and circumstances are right, the Buddha-to-be descends from the Tushita heaven in order to live out his last earthly life.

2. He enters the womb of his mother, Maya, queen to Shuddhodana, king of the Shakyas. Maya dreams of the conception as the entrance into her side of a great white elephant.

3. He takes birth as the prince Siddhartha Gautama in a grove of shala trees at Lumbini, near the Shakya capital of Kapilavastu.

4. Raised as a prince, he gains skill in the various worldly arts, such as literature, war, and rule-of-state.

5. He enjoys the pleasures of a harem, and is married to Yasodhara, who bears him a son, Rahula.

6. He is tormented by encounters with human misery in the forms of a sick man, an old man, and a corpse, and then, to attempt to transcend that misery in the form of a renunciate, he leaves his family and palace behind and becomes a religious mendicant.

7. Both alone, and with other seekers, he undergoes six years of

severe austerities that bring him no closer to enlightenment, but, rather, leave him weak and emaciated.

8. Realizing the futility of asceticism, he abandons his companion-ascetics and eventually accepts a nourishing meal from a milk-maid by the banks of the river Naranjara, near Gaya. Strengthened, he proceeds to the foot of a nearby pipal tree, where, facing east, he sits in meditation, vowing not to rise until he has attained unexcelled, perfect enlightenment.

9. He is assailed by the legions of the Evil One, Mara, who can neither terrify him with conjured demons nor tempt him with his beautiful daughters. In response to Mara's taunt that his victory is hollow because unwitnessed, he touches his right hand to the earth, which rumbles confirmation of his triumph.

10. He sits in meditation through the night, gaining successive realizations of the nature of the myriad of rebirths through which he himself has passed, and of the way in which beings throughout the cosmos, impelled by ignorance and craving, take one unsatisfactory rebirth after another. Finally, at dawn, he realizes that he has eliminated all mental contaminants and need never again be reborn. He has attained the highest possible state, the unexcelled, perfect enlightenment of a buddha, an awakened one.

11. Having rejected the temptation to withhold the Dharma because of its subtlety, he proceeds to Sarnath, near Varanasi, where he "turns the wheel of Dharma" for five ascetic former companions, announcing his discovery of a "middle way" between asceticism and hedonism and of the Four Noble Truths that are the heart of his Dharma: (1) there is suffering; (2) suffering originates from identifiable causes; (3) it is possible to attain a cessation of the origination of suffering, that is, nirvana; and (4) there exists a path that leads to that cessation. Having thus initially promulgated the Dharma, the Buddha embarks on a 45-year career of teaching and organizing his religious community, the sangha.

12. At the age of 80, near the town of Kushinagara, he leaves behind his physical body and passes into *parinirvana*.

Most Buddhist traditions agree on the events that constituted the Buddha's life, but they disagree as to the significance of those events. Theravadins maintain that the Buddha accumulated wisdom and merit through countless lives before his final one, but that when he took birth he was still a buddha-to-be, a bodhisattva, and that only under the pipal tree near Gaya did he actually become a buddha. Before that, he was a great but still imperfect human being, whose doubts and struggles were genuine.

Most Mahayana traditions, on the other hand, are docetic, maintaining that the Buddha attained enlightenment prior to his final birth, and that his life as Shakyamuni was simply a drama he staged to demonstrate the way in which beings might attain the same perfect enlightenment that he had. Futhermore, while the Buddha's *parinirvana* marks for Theravadins his definitive withdrawal from the worldly scene, it is for Mahayanists merely the illusory death of a particular apparition body, or a nirmanakaya. The Buddha continues to exist, his quintessence being his omniscient mind, the dharmakaya. His compassion toward suffering beings is skillfully expressed through his occasional generation of other apparition bodies, and through his appearance to spiritually advanced beings as an enjoyment body, or a sambhogakaya.

Finally, of course, there is considerable disagreement over what the Buddha actually taught during his 45-year career. Theravadins hold that only those *suttas* contained in the Pali canon were taught, while Mahayanists accept that the Buddha taught not only those sutras accepted by the Theravadins (or "Hinayanists"), but also the sutras and tantras that contain various Mahayana doctrines and practices. His non-tantric Mahayana teachings—following the explanation in the *Samdhinirmocana Sutra*—are divided by Tibetans into "three turnings of the Dharma-wheel." These three turnings, in which the Buddha set forth doctrines of varying complexity for beings of varying needs and abilities, provide the fundamental doctrinal structures that are applied to the special practices of tantra, of which the *Kalachakra* is one. The doctrines and practices entailed by the three turnings of the Dharma-wheel can best be understood against the background of the general characteristics of the Buddhist vision of the operation of the cosmos, and the religious and philosophical assumptions that inform that vision.

BASIC BUDDHIST ASSUMPTIONS

Fundamentally, according to the Buddhist vision, the cosmos is twofold, structured so that sentient beings can experience only two

possibilities: samsara, or cyclic existence, and nirvana, or extinction of suffering. Samsara is an individual's continuous series of
more or less unsatisfactory rebirths. These rebirths range from the
excruciating torments of the hells, to the desiccation and starvation
of the hungry ghost realm, to the fear, greed and violence of animal
existence, to the ambiguities and possibilities of human life, to the
nearly unimaginable power, pleasure, and longevity of existence in
the god realms. Despite the differences in the experiences of each
of these realms, all have cerain characteristics in common: whatever their duration, they are temporary conditions, for the greatest
pleasure eventually will give way to pain.

Furthermore, birth into the various realms is under the control
not of one's conscious wishes, but of the impelling power of past
actions, or karma, of body, speech, and mind, and all of these
actions have been fundamentally defiled by ignorance, selfishness,
and craving. As long as one is ignorant of the ultimate nature of
oneself and all phenomena—that being selflessness, emptiness,
and nonsubstantiality—one will continue to grasp at the existence
of a phantom self. As long as one believes in a self, one will
continue to crave the pleasures of that self and to avert what threat-
ens that self. Craving and aversion are the basis of desire and anger,
which in turn are the basis of all other defilements (*kleshas*) that
color one's actions and impel one into one or the other samsaric
realm.

Because samsaric suffering has an identifiable cause—craving
rooted in ignorant self-grasping—it is, in principle, possible that a
being can transcend samsara, for a cause is that factor in the
absence of which an effect does not occur. If ignorant craving is the
cause of continued rebirth in samsara, then the removal of that
ignorant craving should entail the negation of its usual effect,
rebirth.

Thus, nirvana, the extinction of suffering, must be possible. Its
actual attainment is effected by the development of the realization
that neither oneself nor anything else exists permanently, independently, or inherently. Things only "exist" in dependence on causes
and conditions, and therefore are empty of the metaphysical substance we instinctively attribute to them. When one's mental continuum has, through constant meditation, been thoroughly imbued with the understanding of the way phenomena actually exist,

one no longer craves the pleasures or avoids the pains of the "self," for that self is known now to be a phantom, a mere projection on the transient aggregates, or skandhas, that make up what we usually call a "person." In the absence of craving, one no longer possesses the direct cause of rebirth in samsara. When one's understanding of emptiness is so thorough that even the subtlest defilements have been eliminated, one attains nirvana, a condition entirely beyond suffering.

This Buddhist vision of the operation of the cosmos centers, above all, on the nature and destiny of the mind, and it is based on certain assumptions about the mind that need to be spelled out. The first, and perhaps most fundamental, is encoded in the opening words of the *Dhammapada*:

All that we are is a result of
what we have thought:
it is founded on our thoughts,
it is made up of our thoughts.

The mind, which is not a substance or a "thing," but a series of cognitive acts, is the basis of virtually everything that comes about in the cosmos. On the most obvious, psychological level, our mental acts and patterns set up dispositions to feel, think, speak, and behave in various manners consonant with those established acts and patterns. Furthermore, the "seeds" which are "implanted" in the mental continuum by various acts have the power to serve as the cooperative conditions for our encounter with various external circumstances, our taking of particular types of rebirth, and even the existence of the world-environment that we experience in common with other beings of similar karmic background. Mind, therefore, is the most important creative force in the universe, the basis not only of our sorrows and joys, of our failures and successes, but of the very environment that is the stage for our spiritual drama.

Thus, in Buddhism, the mental and physical are far less radically disassociated than they are in the post-Cartesian Western tradition. Notably, it is a fundamental and vital Buddhist assumption that the mind is capable of affecting and altering the physical to an extraordinary degree. When the mind's capacity to create its world is under the control of defiled ignorance, the result is samsara, cyclic existence; when it is under the control of the wisdom that realizes emptiness, the result ultimately will be nirvana. The mind's destiny (and, finally, the destiny of the universe), thus depends quite simply on the way in which the mind is conditioned—and as human beings we have the capacity to condition our minds as we choose.

There may be in Buddhism a considerable overlap between the mental and physical realms, but they are *not* identical. Indeed, the mental and physical represent radically different types of phenomena, capable of indirect mutual influence, but neither one capable of acting as the "material cause" (*upadana hetu*) of the other. A moment of mind, therefore, only can be preceded by a moment of mind. If this is the case, and if mind can arise neither from matter nor *ex nihilo*, then a multiplicity of rebirths must be possible, for if we trace our mental series back to the moment of the conception of this life, that first mind-moment must have a cause that is mental, and that cause only can have occurred in some previous life. Similarly, if we follow our mental series forward until death, we can be certain that mental existence will continue—in still another samsaric body if we have not eliminated ignorant craving, as an enlightened being if we have. This dualism, combined with the assumption that there are regular causal relations between particular mental acts and particular resultant mental, physical, and environmental occurrences, provides the metaphysical basis for belief that there really does exist the round of rebirths that we call samsara.

The belief that nirvana is attainable may be encouraged if one posits a multiplicity of rebirths, since the extraordinary mental discipline necessary for transcending samsara seems out of reach for most humans over the course of a single lifetime. At the same time, nirvana's attainment is not dependent on the existence of past and future lives. Attainment of nirvana only requires that mental acts have consequences regular enough that we can predict and control them, and that the mind be of a nature such that its defilements are not intrinsic to it. The latter is the most important, for if the mind is fundamentally and permanently defiled, all our meditative exertions of a hundred lifetimes will not enable us to transcend samsara.

It is, in fact, the Buddhist assumption that the mind is *not* intrinsically defiled. Although it has acquired defiled properties, its natural function is the clear cognition of objects as they actually exist. Even though the mind has been beginninglessly conditioned to distorted cognition, both distorted cognition and the defile-ments to which such cognition gives rise are adventitious. Reli-giously, the most basic and important distorted cognition is that which involves belief in a metaphysically substantial self. Such a belief, whether conscious or unconscious, entails craving pleasure for the self, hence grasping for that which gives pleasure and aversion to that which gives pain. The undistorted cognition that is the "antidote" to belief in self is the understanding that neither the "person" nor any other phenomenon is or has a metaphysically substantial self—i.e., that the person and all other phenomena are empty. A mind conditioned to the realization of the emptiness of all phenomena no longer craves the pleasures of the self, and thus no longer contains the condition necessary for further samsaric rebirth.

Thus, the cogency of the concepts of both samsara and nirvana rests in large part on an acceptance of the extraordinary impor-tance accorded in Buddhism to the power of the mind. When conditioned ignorantly, the mind is capable of giving rise to afflic-tion after affliction in life after life. However, when conditioned by wisdom, the mind is capable of utterly destroying the basis of suffering and thereby assuring one of the attainment of the eternal, unexcelled happiness of nirvana.

Most contemporary scientists, of course, tend to doubt that the mind can affect matters to such a degree for either good or ill. There is the assumption that we are not responsible for "chance" occurrences—let alone for the existence of our environment—nor are we capable of entirely eliminating all sources of mental dissatis-faction. Our minds simply do not have that much power. Scientific scepticism relies basically on externally observable data and assumptions about what is "normal" in human psychology. Bud-dhist beliefs, however, are rooted, at least in part, on "subjective" observations made during the course of extraordinary mental experiences.

Each of these epistemologies involves potential weaknesses, for an epistemology that accepts the evidence of extraordinary experi-ences sacrifices the relative certainties enjoyed by those who admit hard data and a "normal" range of experiences; while those who admit only the normal will sacrifice finding that in the final analy-sis the ordinary may best be understood from the perspective of

the extra-ordinary. In any case, we will not weigh here the strengths
and weaknesses of either the Buddhist or the more sceptical epistemologies, but content ourselves with pointing out that they are
considerably different, that the mind is accorded much greater
importance in the Buddhist tradition and that, indeed, it is Buddhist assumptions about the mind that form the very basis of the
Dharma expounded in the three turnings of the wheel.

A final important assumption that underlies the Tibetan belief
in the Buddha's three turnings of the Dharma-wheel is the notion
that the Buddha, in dealing with sentient beings, was fundamentally motivated by compassion, and specifically by the desire to aid
beings spiritually to the best of his ability. The intelligence and
dispositions of beings vary greatly, however, so a teaching that is
spiritually efficacious for one type of person may not be so for
another. As a result, through his skill-in-means (*upaya kaushalya*), the
Buddha tailored his message to the audience he was addressing.
Superficially, therefore, there might be contradictions between the
doctrines preached before one audience and those preached
before another, whose capacities differed. In fact, however, all the
Buddha's teachings, whether of definitive or merely provisional
meaning, were intended to be spiritually effective, and all were
based on the "four seals" that are considered the heart of the
Buddhist view of life: (1) all produced phenomena are impermanent; (2) all contaminated entities are suffering; (3) all phenomena
(*dharmas*) whatsoever are selfless; (4) nirvana is peace.

THE THREE TURNINGS OF THE DHARMA-WHEEL

According to the "three-wheel" explanation of the Buddha's
teaching favored by Tibetan Buddhists, the first-turning of the
Dharma-wheel began with the Buddha's first post-enlightenment
discourse at Sarnath. There he taught the middle path and the
Four Noble Truths to his former ascetic companions. Other texts
acknowledged by Tibetan tradition as belonging to the first turning include the *Vinayavastu* (which is concerned with ethical and
disciplinary matters), the *Smrtyupasthana Sutra* (dealing with mindfulness of the body, feelings, mind, and mental phenomena), and
the *Lalitavistara* (a biography of the Buddha). Also included,

though largely unavailable in Tibetan translation, are the various sutras accepted as authoritative by the Theravadin tradition.

The philosophical position espoused by first-turning scriptures may best be described as "realistic," for although the Buddha steadfastly insisted that all products were impermanent and all phenomena selfless, he did maintain that provisional reality could be granted to the phenomena into which one analyzed the everyday world. This realism ultimately emerged in the two Hinayana philosophical schools, the Vaibhashika and Sautrantika. The Vaibhashikas—more or less synonymous with the Sarvastivadins—had their position expounded in such works as Vasumitra's *Mahavibhasha* and Vasubandhu's *Abhidharmakosha*. They upheld the true existence of external objects, and the substantial existence of the three times: past, present, and future. Also basically realistic were the Sautrantikas. However, their doctrines, such as those contained in Vasubandhu's auto-commentary to the *Abhidharmakosha*, arose in part as a reaction against the excessive realism of the Vaibhashikas. Sautrantikas denied the substantial existence of past and future, and generally reduced the number of entities granted true existence. Their position approached that of nominalism, but they still were realists, for they continued to assert the true existence of external objects.

The second turning of the Dharma-wheel began with the Buddha's espousal at Vulture Peak near Rajagriha of the various Perfection of Wisdom (*prajnaparamita*) sutras, which range in length from a hundred thousand verses to the single syllable "a." Among the best known and most concise of the texts are the *Heart of Perfect Wisdom Sutra (Prajnaparamita Hrdaya Sutra)* and the *Diamond-cutter Sutra (Vajraccheddika Sutra)*. Also included by the dGe lug pas in the second turning are the *Lankavatara Sutra*, the *Avatamsaka Sutra*, the *Samadhiraja Sutra*, the various sutras of the *Ratnakuta* collection, and a number of sutras that discuss the concept of *tathagatagarbha*, the womb or embryo of the *tathagata*—often rendered loosely as "buddha-nature"—that is the mental potential of all beings.

The basic philosophical position espoused by the Buddha during the second turning is that there is no entity or phenomenon whatsoever whose ultimate nature is not emptiness, or shunyata, because there is no entity or phenomenon whose existence is not dependent on extrinsic causes and conditions, and on the labels

and categories either deliberately or instinctively imposed by the
mind. This radical emphasis on emptiness issued eventually in the
Madhyamika, one of the two basic philosophical schools of the
Mahayana. The fundamental commentary for all Madhyamikas is
the *Madhyamakakarika* of Nagarjuna. Later Madhyamikas themselves divided into two schools. The Svatantrikas, who included
Bhavaviveka, Shantarakshita and Kamalashila, favored syllogistic
forms of argumentation and granted that, at least conventionally, it
could be said that phenomena exist by way of their own characteristics. The Prasangikas, who included Buddhapalita, Chandrakirti
and Shantideva, favored the *reductio ad absurdum* as a method of
argumentation and would not concede that phenomena exist by
way of their own characteristics even conventionally, for conventionally they exist as dependently originated (*pratitya samutpada*)
from extrinsic causes and conditions.

The third turning of the Dharma-wheel took place at Vaishali
and other places frequented by the Buddha. Like the second turning, the wheel was turned a third time for the sake of bodhisattvas,
those who had vowed to attain enlightenment for the sake of all
sentient beings. The first wheel had been turned largely for the
sake of those whose primary concern was their own liberation from
samsara. The basic sutra of the third wheel is the *Samdhinirmochana*,
which actually introduces the classification of the Buddha's teaching into three wheels. Also included in the third turning are some
of the sutras that discuss the concept of *tathagatagarbha*.

The third turning is sometimes called the turning of "fine
distinctions," because its main philosophical concern is to modify
the realism and the *apparent* nihilism of the second turning by
distinguishing those phenomena that ultimately exist from those
that do not. Ultimate existence is ascribed to dependent phenomena (*paratantra*) and their final, established nature (*parinishpanna*),
emptiness. Ultimate non-existence is ascribed to imaginary (*pari-
kalpita*) entities and attributes that are mentally imputed to dependent phenomena. The outgrowth of the third turning was the
second major Mahayana philosophical school, the Chittamatra, or
"Mind-Only," which is roughly synonymous with Yogachara and
Vijnanavada.

Chittamatrins following scripture, who included Vasubandhu
and his brother Asanga, denied the independent existence of

external objects, posited a storehouse consciousness, or *alaya vijnana*, underlying the sensory and mental consciousnesses accepted by other schools, and generally adopted a metaphysical position that is akin to subjective idealism in the West. Although religiously, like the Madhyamikas, the Chittamatrins were primarily concerned with analyzing the way in which our mental imputations ascribe to phenomena a reality they do not ultimately possess, and thereby act as the basis of samsaric suffering.

Chittamatrins following reasoning, who included Dignaga, Dharmakirti, and Dharmottara, were concerned primarily with epistemological matters: types of valid cognition (*pramana*), rules of inference, etc. Their works have had a tremendous impact on all later Buddhist philosophy, because they established rigorously the forms in which philosophical discussion most meaningfully could take place.

Although the *Samdhinirmocana Sutra*, a Chittamatrin work, maintains that sutras of the third turning are of definitive meaning (*nitartha*), while those of the first two turnings have merely provisional meaning (*neyartha*), virtually all Tibetan traditions of interpretation assert that the second turning is, in fact, the definitive one, and the first and third merely provisional. This is because, for the most part, Tibetan traditions consider the Madhyamika to be the highest philosophical expression of the Buddha's Dharma, and the Perfection of Wisdom sutras of the second turning most closely prefigure the Madhyamika.

It is important to note that although there are gradations of subtlety among Buddhist philosophical schools, "lower" schools are not considered false so much as they are provisional. Thus, in the dGe lug pas view, the Vaibashika position prepares the way for the Sautrantika, the Sautrantika for the Chittamatra, the Chittamatra for the Svatantrika Madhyamika, and the Svatantrika Madhyamika for the Prasangika Madyamika. The Prasangika may represent the most advanced point of view, but it will be better understood against the backgound of the "lower" schools. Thus, the four schools represent a variety of possible philosophical positions, and an understanding of all of them will help to improve one's philosophical acuity, regardless of which one one actually follows.

THE FIVE PATHS TO LIBERATION

The ultimate purpose of philosophy in Buddhism is liberation. We must, therefore, give at least a brief accounting of the spiritual paths believed taught by the Buddha. The "eightfold noble path" taught in the first sermon at Sarnath entails the cultivation of right view, right thought, right speech, right action, right livelihood, right effort, right mindfulness, and right concentration. Theravada tradition, particulary as encoded in the *Visuddhimagga* of Buddhaghosa, stresses the successive cultivation of morality, concentration, and wisdom.

However, in the scheme accepted by virtually all Sanskritic and Tibetan traditions, the Buddha taught five paths, which could be traversed by the members of any of the three classes of disciples: shravakas, pratyekabuddhas, and bodhisattvas. Shravakas and pratyekabuddhas (to whom the first turning of the Dharma-wheel was primarily directed) are considered to be Hinayana disciples, and concerned primarily with attaining their own liberation from samsara. Bodhisattvas (to whom the second and third turnings of the Dharma-wheel were primarily directed) are dedicated to attaining full enlightenment, that highest degree of knowledge, compassion, and skill on the basis of which they may give aid to suffering sentient beings. Of the five paths, the first two, those of accumulation and application, are considered mundane; the final three, those of seeing, development, and no-more-training, are considered to be transmundane, for on them one is no longer an ordinary being, or *pritagjana*, but an arya, or "noble one," irreversibly destined for enlightenment.

Each philosophical school explains the progress of the three types of disciples along the five paths differently. According to the Prasangika Madhyamika, the path followed by a Hinayana shravaka or pratyekabuddha is roughly as follows. Having generated a sincere and spontaneous desire to be free utterly of the fetters of samsara, the disciple enters the first path, that of accumulation (*sambhara marga*). On this path, the disciple cultivates in particular the four mindfulnesses (of body, feelings, mind, and mental phenomena), and develops mental quiescence. On the second path, that of application (*prayoga marga*), the disciple is devoted chiefly to gaining a profound conceptual insight into the Four Noble Truths, which are divided into sixteen "aspects." At the conclusion of the path of application, the disciple, for the first time, combines mental quiescence with insight in examining the truths, and gains a direct, non-conceptual realization of them. At this point, arya status and the path of seeing (*darshana marga*)are attained. The disciple is enabled by this direct realization, particularly of the aspects of selflessness and emptiness, to begin actually to eliminate defilements. On the first two paths, the disciple had only succeeded in suppressing them. In the sixteen brief "moments" of the path of seeing the disciple uproots various gross defilements. On the path of development (*bhavana marga*), the disciple uproots defilements of increasing subtlety, until there are no defilements left to eliminate. The disciple thus enters the path of no-more-training (*ashaiksha marga*), and becomes an arahant, free from samsara.

A bodhisattva, having generated a sincere and spontaneous desire to attain full enlightenment for the sake of all sentient beings, enters the Mahayana path of accumulation. Here the bodhisattva cultivates the four mindfulnesses and develops mental quiescence, then passes on to the path of application, where she or he strives for a conceptual insight into emptiness. When quiescence and insight are combined in examining emptiness, the bodhisattva attains a direct, non-conceptual realization of emptiness, and thus becomes an arya, on the path of seeing. The path of seeing corresponds to the first of the ten *bhumis*, i.e. stages, levels, or grounds said to be traversed by a bodhisattva. The other nine *bodhisattva* stages are coextensive with the path of development, during the course of which the disciple completely eliminates not only the defilements that are obstacles to liberation but even the traces of defilement, which are obstacles to full enlightenment. When the path of development is completed, the disciple is ready to enter the path of no-more-training; this marks the attainment of full enlightenment, the dharmakaya, sambhogakaya, and nirmanakaya of an omniscient, compassionate, and powerful buddha.

There are both similarities and differences between Hinayana and Mahayana paths. On the one hand—so Prasangika Madhyamikas maintain—shravakas, pratyekabuddhas, and bodhisattvas all attain the path of seeing through a direct cognition of the same object: the emptiness of inherent existence characteristic of all phenomena. All Buddhist disciples, thus, attain the same *wisdom* that is the requisite basis for the elimination of defilements; thus all are capable at the very least of gaining liberation from samsara.

On the other hand, bodhisattvas, because they are motivated altruistically, employ more extensive *methods*, and, through their practice of such perfections, or *paramitas*, as generosity, morality, patience, zeal and concentration, accumulate far greater merit than do Hinayana disciples. As a result, they are able to eliminate not just obstacles to liberation, but also obstacles to omniscience. Furthermore, whereas Hinayana disciples are capable "merely" of attaining the trans-samsaric state of arahantship, bodhisattvas are capable of attaining the three bodies or *kayas* of a Buddha.

It is a central teaching of the second turning of the Dharma-wheel that buddhist practice finally issues in a single result: the full enlightenment of buddhahood. Thus, although arahantship does mark a transcendence of samsara, it is not an end in itself, but a way station on the road to buddhahood. Sooner or later, an arahant must stir from the individual transcendent bliss and take up personally the responsibility for helping to free others, too. In short, the arahant must eventually become a bodhisattva, and ultimately a buddha, for the buddha ultimately taught but one vehicle (*ekayana*), and that was the Bodhisattva Vehicle.

TANTRA IN GENERAL

According to the interpretive scheme adopted by most Tibetan Buddhists, the Bodhisattva Vehicle, or Mahayana, has two divisions. One is the long, gradual ascent toward enlightenment described above; this is known as the Sutra Vehicle or Perfection Vehicle. The other is the rapid, arduous approach provided by the esoteric techniques of the vehicle known as the Mantra Vehicle, Tantra Vehicle, or Vajra Vehicle. A bodhisattva following the Perfection Vehicle can be expected to require three "great countless eons" to traverse the five paths (discussed earlier) of accumulation, application, seeing, development, and no-more-training, by gradually perfecting generosity, morality, patience, and other virtues, and gradually eliminating defilements and their traces through an ever more thorough comprehension of emptiness, i.e., of the selflessness of persons and phenomena.

A bodhisattva following the Mantra Vehicle is able, through the special methods provided by the tantras, to shorten drastically the traversal of the five paths. If the disciple is a skilled practitioner of the highest of the four levels of tantra, the *Anuttara* or "unsurpassed" Yoga tantra, the five paths can be traversed in the course of a single lifetime. Most Tibetan traditions of explanation take the position that a bodhisattva cannot, in fact, attain Buddhahood only through following the Perfection Vehicle. That vehicle may take the disciple to the very end of the path of development, to the tenth bodhisattva *bhumi*, but in order to achieve buddhahood, that being must enter the Mantra Vehicle; specifically the disciple must complete the practices of the *Anuttara* yoga tantra. In these traditions, it is assumed that Shakyamuni Buddha achieved enlightenment through practicing *Anuttara* Yoga tantra; that he taught the *Anuttara* Yoga tantra as the final, indispensible door to enlightenment; and that all previous and subsequent enlightened beings have reached buddhahood through the *Anuttara* Yoga tantra.

Before we discuss the distinctive features of the Tantra Vehicle that set it apart from the Perfection Vehicle, it is important to stress the continuities that exist between the two vehicles.

In the first place, both are divisions of the Mahayana, so a tantric practitioner, no less than a "conventional" bodhisattva, must be motivated primarily by the intention to attain enlightenment for the sake of all sentient beings. Indeed, the arduousness and subtlety of tantric practice require, if anything, even greater compassion as their driving force. Thus, although not *on* the Perfection Vehicle, a tantric practitioner is still a bodhisattva, and consequently strives not only to attain the mundane and transmundane powers or *siddhi* that come from tantric practice, but also to perfect the generosity, morality, patience, zeal, concentration, and wisdom stressed in "perfection" practice. Futhermore, just as the object of a wisdom consciousness was the same for Hinayana and Perfection Vehicle practitioners—all phenomena's emptiness of inherent existence—so is the object the same for Perfection Vehicle and tantric practitioners. "Tantric" emptiness differs from that cognized on the Perfection Vehicle only from the point of view of the cognizing subject, which in tantra is an extermely subtle level of mind.

The most important—indeed, the defining—characteristic of

tantra is the practice of *deity yoga*. Broadly speaking, deity yoga involves the visualization, or imagination, of oneself with the bodily form and mental attributes of the buddha one someday will become. This practice is sometimes known as "taking the fruit as the path."

Specifically, deity yoga involves a consciousness, cognizing emptiness, that appears in the form of a deity. A divine appearance that is empty of inherent existence is said to be the coincidence of wisdom and method. Thus, whereas on the Perfection Vehicle, wisdom and method are mutually reinforcing but never simultaneous or substantially identical, in tantra they are simultaneous aspects of one and the same consciousness.

It is the *method* involved that makes deity yoga distinctive. The wisdom whose accumulation will result in a buddha's dharmakaya does not differ from one vehicle to the next. Rather, it is the visualization of a divine form, the basic method of deity yoga, that is the only real way in which one can attain sufficient merit to produce the two types of "form bodies" of a buddha: the enjoyment body or sambhogakaya, and the emanation bodies or nirmanakaya. This is said to be so because, in the final analysis, one cannot achieve a particular result from a cause that differs in aspect from that result. Thus, one only will attain the bodies of a buddha by simulating them. Only deity yoga provides such simulations of divinity, so only the Tantra Vehicle, of which deity yoga is the defining characteristic, can carry one directly to buddhahood.

If deity yoga is the heart of tantra, then the "tantric view of life" has nothing to do with eroticism, ritualism, or the exaltation of the ordinary. Rather, it involves primarily *imagination* and *transformation*. Tantric practitioners are instructed repeatedly to have "divine pride," that is, to hold a view of themselves and the world as the divine mind, body, and environment that will eventually be enjoyed. Thus, they are instructed constantly to see themselves as possessing the mental and physical attributes of a particular form of the Buddha; to see their environment as the mandala, or divine residence—usually a mansion—of the deity; to bless and purify ordinary enjoyments, such as food, and see them as a divine nectar instilling uncontaminated wisdom; and to see their actions as the actions of a buddha, who uses both wrath and gentleness to fulfill the spiritual needs of sentient beings. In addition, other sentient beings may be seen as deities in one's mandala, and all sounds may be heard as mantras.

The sort of "dress-rehearsal for enlightenment" involved in deity yoga and divine pride is neither presumptuous nor futile, because (a) the elements, aggregates, attitudes, and drives that comprise an ordinary person are ultimately empty, and thus capable of transformation in any number of ways, and (b) the mind is the supreme transformative agent in the universe, for as it is conditioned, so, ultimately, is the world conditioned. Inasmuch as "all we are is a result of what we have thought," then conditioning the mind to divine pride is a form of imagination that ultimately can effect a transformation of the ordinary into the divinity that is imagined. For example, the five aggregates (or five defilements) can be transformed into the five types of wisdom of the five tathagatas, or "dhyani buddhas," who head the different tantric lineages; the elements can be transformed into their consorts, sense organs into bodhisattvas; action-organs into protectors. In short, because reality follows thought, imagination can be transformative.

Although deity yoga is tantra's defining characteristic, there are a number of other unique features of tantra that should be singled out. First, successful tantric practice—far more than other Buddhist practices—requires a very close working relationship between disciple and master. A tantric master must be both knowledgeable and skillful in the various meditative techniques, and must be sensitive to the various problems the disciple may encounter. A tantric disciple must be confident of the master's qualifications, and unquestioning in the fulfillment of the instructions that the master has given—for the subtlety and danger of tantra is such that capriciousness or disobedience can lead to dire results.

This subtlety and danger of tantra is based in part on the fact that tantric practitioners seek to utilize and transform—rather than suppress—such defilements as desire and anger. Utilizing and transforming defilements is a delicate and complex process, in which the risk of self-deception or madness is quite real—hence the need for guidance by an experienced master.

Second, because tantric practice aims not at the transcendence but the transformation of our ordinary elements, aggregates, attitudes, and drives, tantric symbolism and imagery is both rich and striking—and often unsettling. Tantric deities usually have many arms and often more than one face, for only such complexity can convey the virtual universe of meanings contained in the enlightened state of which the deity is an exemplar. Tantric deities often are depicted as wrathful, but only because anger, like other defilements, can be used for spiritual purposes, e.g., in expressing an adamantine determination to rid one's mind of all impediments to successful practice. Tantric deities often are depicted in sexual union with an ecstatic consort, which signifies both that desire can be transmuted for use on the spiritual path, and that tantra in general is a path that *unites* method and wisdom, appearance and emptiness, bliss and non-dualistic awareness.

Third, tantra assumes the existence of a great many different types of deities. These include such mundane entities as earth-spirits, nagas, directional guardians, and the various Hindu deities; and such trans-mundane entities as wrathful Dharma-protectors, the *dakas* and *dakinis* that aid one's meditation, and the enlightened deities that are manifestations of the Buddha, and whom one invokes or identifies oneself with in deity yoga.

Fourth, tantra presupposes and utilizes an alternative vision of human physiology, describing mental and material processes in terms of chakras (vital centers, lit. "wheels"); channels (*nadis*); wind (prana, sometimes described as "vital energy," and related to the breath); drops (*bindu*) of semen and blood derived from the parents; and the subtle mind.

There are six major chakras, located at the crown of the head, forehead, throat, heart, navel, and genitals. There are three major channels, in the center, right, and left of the body, just forward of the spine. (There are six channels if the body is divided into upper and lower halves.) The right and left channels intersect the central channel at the chakras. The channels are conduits for the various winds and drops that are said to be the actual basis of our physical functions and concomitants of our states of consciousness. On the most fundamental level, mind is associated with the winds and drops, but although affected by their location and movement, it also can direct them. In the ultimate stage of tantric practice, buddhahood is achieved in part through directing all winds into the central channel and purifying the drops there. Meditations involving the chakras, channels, winds, and drops are generally performed within the context of deity yoga. The chakras, channels, winds, and drops are not believed to be equivalent to processes known to Western physiology, but to be the subtler basis of those processes. Thus, tantric theory does not contradict the scientific view of the body so much as it supplements it.

Finally, tantra is set apart by the fact that one cannot practice the yoga of a particular deity unless one receives an initiation, or empowerment (abhisheka) from a qualified master. The master must have received his or her initiation in an unbroken lineage that stretches back to the Buddha himself, as well as having completed a retreat devoted to the deity in question. In the course of an initiation, the disciple makes various supplications, offerings, and pledges; in turn, the master, in the form of the deity, introduces the disciple to the mandala, mantras, and symbolism of the particular tantra. In the long term, the various rituals entailed by the initiation empower the disciple to accomplish various mundane and trans-mundane goals, the highest of which is, of course, buddhahood. In the short term, an initiation empowers a disciple to practice the sadhana of a particular deity.

A sadhana, the context in which deity yoga usually is practiced, involves, at the very least, the following elements: (1) taking as one's spiritual refuge the Buddha, Dharma and Sangha; (2) generation of the altruistic intention to attain enlightenment or *bodhicitta*; (3) cultivation of immeasurable love, compassion, sympathetic joy, and equanimity toward other beings; (4) reduction of one's ordinary appearance to emptiness; (5) generation of oneself in the form of the deity, pure in body, speech, and mind; (6) absorption of the actual deity or gnosis being, (*jnanasattva*), who is called from its abode, into the imagined deity or pledge being, (*samayasattva*); (7) initiation by the deities; (8) repetition of mantras that effect the welfare of sentient beings and symbolize the deity's speech; and (9) dissolution of the divine form into emptiness—from which one usually arises again as the deity, often in simpler form.

Sadhanas also usually involve a variety of symbolic and actual offerings; hand-gestures known as mudras; the use of such ritual implements as the vajra, bell, and hand-drum (*damaru*); and additional visualizations, e.g., of the deity's mandala, or divine residence. The visualizations and various ritual acts in a tantric sadhana require extraordinary discipline and powers of concentration. Indeed, among the three basic Buddhist trainings—in morality, concentration, and wisdom—it is concentration, or samadhi, for which tantra provides techniques markedly superior to those of other vehicles.

KRIYA, CHARYA, AND YOGA TANTRA

Most of the tantric practices that have been handed down through the Indian and Tibetan traditions are assumed to have been taught by the Buddha himself, either in his nirmanakaya form as Shakyamuni; in the form of his basic tantric manifestation, Vajradhara; or in the guise of the deity with which a particular tantra is concerned, such as Mahavairochana, Guhyasamaja, or Kalachakra. The Buddha's promulgations of the tantras is not specifically associated with one of the three turnings of the Dharma-wheel, but the centrality of emptiness to deity yoga points up an implicit connection with the second turning. Indeed, it is believed that when the Buddha took the form of Kalachakra to preach the *Kalachakra Tantra* at Shridhanyakataka, in south India, at precisely the same time he manifested as Shakyamuni at Vulture Peak near Rajagriha and taught the Perfection of Wisdom sutras.

The tantras taught by the Buddha are divided variously. The rNying ma pa (Nyingmapa) tradition of Tibetan Buddhism, for instance, counts six different classes. The most common division is into four: *Kriya* (action), *Charya* (performance), *Yoga* (union), and *Anuttara Yoga* (supreme union). In the most general terms, these classes are said to reflect the mental capacity and religious propensities of their practitioners. Thus, *Kriya* tantra is set forth for those of somewhat lesser mental capacity, and although it involves deity yoga and presupposes a certain degreee of meditative prowess, it places greater emphasis on external purification and ritual action than on internal yoga. *Charya* tantra strikes a balance between external performance and internal yoga. Yoga tantra emphasizes internal yoga more strongly than external ritual. *Anuttara* Yoga tantra, which is set forth only for the most intelligent and dedicated of practitioners, is concerned almost exclusively with complex internal yogic processes.

The relative intensity and effectiveness of the four classes also sometimes is expressed in terms of the relationship between a man and a woman: *Kriya* tantra is an exchange of looks; *Charya* tantra is an exchange of smiles; Yoga tantra is holding hands or embracing; and *Anuttara* Yoga tantra is sexual union. This last, as noted above, is a powerful metaphor for the ultimate integration of complementary qualities that is buddhahood.

Practices in the *Kriya* tantra are chiefly divided according to three trans-mundane families, or lineages: the Tathagata, the Lotus, and the Vajra. Manjushri is the best-known deity associated with the Tathagata family; Avalokiteshvara is best-known with the Lotus; and Vajrapani with the Vajra. Disciples will be initiated into the practices of one or the other of these depending on whether they will benefit most from association with the wisdom, compassion or power of the Buddha. Generally speaking, *Kriya* tantra initiations are subdivided into only two: the water and crown initiations. Those initiated into the *Kriya* tantra must uphold the vows taken by bodhisattvas, but, because they have not received the initiation of the vajra master, they are not bound to uphold the vows particular to tantric practitioners.

Kriya tantra practices, or sadhanas, are generally divided into yoga with signs, or *sanimitta*, and yoga without signs, or *animitta*. Yoga with signs is concerned chiefly with establishing a clear visualization of the body of the deity. This process involves visualizing the deity in the mandala before one; then, with regard to oneself, contemplating the deity in the form of emptiness, the sound of the mantra, the letters of the mantra, the body, the seal-blessing on one's body, and the actual absorption of the deity into oneself so that one possesses the deity's "sign," the coincidence of clear appearance and divine pride. One then practices *pranayama*, or breath control, in order to still the mind and maintain the clarity of one's visualization. On the basis of *pranayama*, one recites the mantra of the deity, concentrating on either the shape or sound of the syllables. For those adept in meditation with recitation, there are meditations without recitation, in which one imagines the mantra as emitted by the luminosity or sound of a flame at one's heart. On the basis of meditation without recitation, one achieves mental quiescence; on the basis of that achievement, one contemplates emptiness. This contemplation, in which awareness of divine sounds and forms is subordinated, is yoga without signs; it can serve to generate a direct realization of emptiness and achievement of the path of seeing.

The *Charya* tantra also is generally divided into practices of the Tathagata, Lotus, and Vajra families. The most important *Charya* tantra is that of Mahavairocana, who belongs to the Tathagata family. The best-known Lotus family deity is Hayagriva (whose tantra was not translated into Tibetan), and the best-known Vajra family deity is, again, Vajrapani. In addition to the water and crown initiations, *Charya* tantra abhishekas include the initiations of the vajra, bell, and name. As in *Kriya* tantra, there is no initiation of the vajra master, so tantric vows need not be upheld; bodhisattva vows, however, must.

Charya tantra practice also is divided into yoga with signs and yoga without signs. Yoga with signs consists of repetition with external and internal branches. External repetition involves visualizing oneself as the deity, e.g., Mahavairocana; visualizing the deity before one; identifying one's mind with a moon disc at the heart of the deity before one; and recitation of the mantra surrounding the deity's heart. Internal repetition involves visualizing oneself as Shakyamuni Buddha, visualizing Mahavairocana on a moon disc at one's heart, imagining one's mind in the form of a moon disc at Mahavairocana's heart, and imagining and repeating the syllables of the deity's mantra. As in *Kriya* tantra all repetition is to be done on the basis of *pranayama*. Yoga without signs in the *Charya* tantra involves simultaneous visualization of oneself in divine form and contemplation of that form's emptiness of inherent existence. Both *Kriya* and *Charya* tantra practices serve as the basis for the eventual attainment of the path of seeing and of various powers, or siddhi, with which one can aid sentient beings.

Yoga tantra includes the practices of four families, the Tathagata, Vajra, Lotus, and Jewel, ruled in turn by the tathagatas Vairocana, Akshobhya, Amitabha, and Ratnasambhava, and appropriate to persons ruled by desire, anger, ignorance and greed, respectively. The basic text of the Yoga tantra is known as the *Tattvasamgraha*. It was expounded by the Buddha in the form of Vairocana, who also is the principal deity of the tantra.

Yoga tantra initiations include the five "lower" initiations, as well as the initiation of the vajra master. Practitioners of Yoga tantra, therefore, are expected to keep both bodhisattva and tantric vows.

The basic procedure of Yoga tantra practice is an attempt to transform one's ordinary body, speech, mind, and actions into a divine body, speech, mind, and actions, chiefly through the application of four "seals," or mudra: the *mahamudra* (great seal), *samayamudra* (pledge seal), *dharmamudra*, and *karmamudra* (action seal). At the outset, one generates oneself in the form of the pledge being (*samayasattva*), e.g., Vairocana, then invokes the gnosis being (*jnanasattva*) from the actual abode, and dissolves the gnosis being into the pledge being. One then applies the four seals. Identifying oneself with the deity and the deity's mind, and symbolizing one's knowledge of the deity's mind (which cognizes emptiness) with a hand symbol, one applies the *samayamudra*; this serves to transform mind, anger, and one's fire element into the perfection of giving, the equalizing wisdom of a buddha, and the omniscient aspect of the dharmakaya. Identifying oneself with the deity and various internal syllables, and symbolizing the speech of the deity by syllables visualized in his body, one applies the *dharmamudra*; this serves to transform speech, ignorance, and one's water element into the perfection of wisdom, the discriminating wisdom of a buddha, and the sambhogakaya. Identifying oneself with the actions of the deity, one applies the *karmamudra*; this transforms one's actions, greed, and wind element into the perfection of zeal, the all-accomplishing wisdom, and the nirmanakaya. Finally, identifying oneself with the deity, whose body is symbolized by a hand gesture, one applies the *mahamudra*; this serves to transform the body, desire, and one's earth element into the mind of enlightenment, or *bodhicitta*, the mirror-like wisdom, and the natural emptiness of the dharmakaya. Further symbolic correspondences are involved, for instance in terms of four mandalas, and each of the seals is applied during one's contemplation of oneself as each of the rulers of the four Yoga tantra families.

In Yoga tantra, unlike in the two lower tantras, one actually can generate a semblance of the divine body that one eventually will assume, and then actually transform one's body into that of a tenth-level bodhisattva or a knowledge-holder (*vidyadhara*). One cannot, however, complete one's transformation into an actual enlightened deity.

ANUTTARA YOGA TANTRA

Although the *Anuttara* Yoga tantra recognizes five "families," headed by Vairocana, Ratnasambhava, Amitabha, Amoghasiddhi, and Akshobhya (with either Vajrasattva or Vajradhara sometimes added as a sixth), these families do not—as they do in the lower tantras—mark off its major divisions. Rather, the *Anuttara* Yoga tantra is divided into "father," or "method," or *daka* tantras, and "mother," or "wisdom," or *dakini* tantras.

Father tantras, which include the practices of Guhyasamaja and Yamantaka, are prescribed as a method for transmuting desire, anger, and ignorance. These concentrate on the generation of the illusory body (*mayadeha*) that will be transformed into the form bodies (sambhogakaya and nirmanakaya) of a buddha when one attains enlightenment. Mother tantras, which include the practices of Chakrasamvara (or Heruka), Hevajra, Vajrayogini, and Kala-chakra, concentrate their attention on the clear light (*prabhasvara*) consciousness that cognizes emptiness, is the indissoluble unity of bliss and emptiness, and will be transformed into the dharmakaya of a buddha when one attains enlightenment. The illusory body and clear light, in turn, are two major factors on the completion stage, the latter of the two stages into which *anuttara* yoga tantra practice is divided.

Initiation into an *Anuttara* Yoga tantra generally entails four basic initiations: a vase initiation (in turn divided into water, crown, vajra, bell, and name initiations), a secret initiation, a wisdom-gnosis initiation, and a "fourth," and highest, initiation. These initiations entail the taking of bodhisattva vows, tantric vows, and specific vows required by each of the five families of tathagatas. *Anuttara* Yoga tantra initiations, unlike those of any other tantra, empower the disciple to undertake certain practices at the completion of which the disciple will attain the unsurpassable, perfect enlightenment of a buddha.

The first of the two levels of *Anuttara* Yoga tantra practice is the generation stage (*utpattikrama*), empowered by the vase initiation. A practitioner on the generation stage is concerned chiefly with developing a clear visualization of him or herself as the deity (usually in sexual union with a consort) at the center of a mandala that contains various levels, doors, and anywhere from a few to hundreds of subsidiary deities. Incidentally, although mandalas are represented two-dimensionally on painted scrolls, they are to be visualized three-dimensionally.

Different activities in the course of a generation-stage sadhana are said to provide the basis for the purification of the basic life-stages. Thus, one's assumption of the deity's dharmakaya (by, e.g., dissolving all appearances into emptiness) is the basis of the purification of death, in the first moment of which consciousness attains a clear light vision. One's assumption of the deity's sambhogakaya (by, e.g., visualizing the syllable from which the divine form is generated) is the basis for the purification of the intermediate state between death and rebirth. One's assumption of the deity's nirmanakaya (by, e.g., generating oneself as the deity) is the basis for the purification of birth, that one need never again take birth in an ordinary body. The actual purification of death, birth, and the intermediate state does not occur until the completion stage, where the production of clear light pre-enacts and purifies death, and production of the illusory body purifies rebirth. One is said to have completed the generation stage and to be ready for the completion stage when one can maintain single-pointed concentration on oneself as the deity at the center of a mandala visualized so clearly that one can see the whites of the eyes of every deity in it.

The practices of the completion stage (*sampannakrama*) are empowered by the secret, wisdom-gnosis, and fourth initiations. At the outset—often within the context of visualizing oneself as the deity in the "simple" (one face and two arm) form—one directs all the winds that generally flow through the left and right channels into the central channel, and brings them together at the heart. Next, one directs one's subtle mind through four levels of "light" (or emptiness, or joy), culminating with the attainment of the "approximating" clear light. With the mind of the approximating clear light as the cooperative condition and the winds (which *are* our subtle body) as the material cause, one generates an "impure" illusory body, a tiny semblance of the divine form one ultimately will have as a buddha. The attainment of the impure illusory body assures the practitioner that enlightenment will be achieved either in this life or immediately after it. By joining the approximating clear light with the impure illusory body, the practitioner purifies the illusory body and gains a clear light that directly realizes emptiness. The final procedure, "union" (*yuganaddha*), frequently involves stacking in the central channel the body's 21,600 "red" (= blood = female) and 21,600 "white" (= semen = male) drops, the joining and purification of which seals one's attainment of the clear light and illusory body, and completes the transformation of one's mind and body into the dharmakaya and sambhogakaya and nirmanakayas of a fully enlightened buddha.

The feature that most clearly distinguishes the *Anuttara* Yoga tantra from the three lower tantras is, of course, the fact that through it, and it alone, one actually traverses both the mundane and trans-mundane bodhisattva paths and attains complete buddhahood. (The generation stage is the path of accumulation, and during the completion stage one traverses the paths of application, seeing, development, and no-more-training.)

It is set apart from the lower tantras in other ways, too. First, it is the only tantra in which one can resort to an actual consort, or *karmamudra*, in the course of practice. When one has attained the impure illusory body, and uses an actual consort, one will attain enlightenment in the course of that very life. If, having attained the impure illusory body, one uses an imagined consort, or *jnanamudra*, one will attain enlightenment immediatedly after death, as did Tsong kha pa, the founder of the dGe lug pas tradition.

Second, *Anuttara* Yoga tantra, like Yoga tantra, has four seals, but the names differ slightly and the meaning differs considerably. Their purpose is to aid one in attaining mental quiescence and realizing emptiness. The *karmamudra* is an actual consort without the usual traditionally prescribed qualities of age, form, training, etc. The *samayamudra* is an actual consort who does have the proper qualities. The *jnanamudra* is an imagined consort. The *mahamudra* involves no consort, but, rather, contemplation of the indivisibility of wisdom and method (or compassion). The seals are, in sequence, for disciples of great, lesser, little, and almost no sexual desire and mental discursiveness.

Third, the indivisibility of wisdom and method, which has already been noted as a general characteristic of tantra, has the particular sense in the *Anuttara* Yoga tantra of a wisdom-consciousness, realizing emptiness, that is indivisible from great bliss (the "method" in this case).

THE KALACHAKRA TANTRA

The Kalachakra Tantra is a mother tantra and, like any *Anuttara* Yoga tantra, teaches practices that can lead directly to buddhahood in the course of a single lifetime. It is not, thus, really "superior" to other *Anuttara* Yoga tantras; *"anuttara"*, after all, means that than which nothing is higher. At the same time, the Kalachakra system contains a number of unique features that set it apart from other *Anuttara* Yoga tantras, and that have led many Tibetan commentators to consider it the very pinnacle of the Buddha's teachings, his most complex and profound statement on both temporal and spiritual matters. The most important of these features can be enumerated as follows.

1. Whereas other *Anuttara* Yoga tantras taught by the Buddha were preserved and transmitted in India, the Kalachakra Tantra while taught in India, was not actually practiced in India before the ninth or tenth century A.D. The reason for this is that the Kalachakra was taught to Suchandra, (or Chandrabhadra), King of the land of Shambhala. Suchandra returned with the tantra to Shambhala, and established there a tradition of its practice. The tantra was not brought back to India until Chilupa sought it out late in the first millenium A.D.

2. Uniquely among the tantras, the Kalachakra has three general divisions: Outer Kalachakra, Inner Kalachakra and Other Kalachakra. Outer Kalachakra refers to yearly and historical timecycles. It deals with various matters of astrology, geomancy, geography, history, and eschatology; it is said to correspond generally to the external environment and cosmos in which we live. No other tantra discusses these topics in any detail. Inner Kalachakra refers to the time-cycle of breaths taken by a person in a day. It includes one's aggregates, elements, attitudes, and drives, as well as the chakras, channels, winds, drops, and mind that are the basis of the tantric vision of the "person." Outer and Inner Kalachakra are the basis that is to be purified by spiritual practice. Other Kalachakra is that which purifies the Outer and Inner Kalachakras: the stages of generation and completion.

3. Other *Anuttara* Yoga tantras have four initiations, the first of which generally empowers one to practice the generation stage, and the latter three of which generally empower one to practice the

completion stage. The Kalachakra system involves eleven initiations. One is empowered to practice the generation stage by the
seven initiations analogous to events in childhood; these are called
the water, crown, crown pendant, vajra and bell, conduct, name,
and permission initiations. One is empowered to practice the completion stage by the four "higher" and the four "higher than high"
initiations, each of which consists of a vase, secret, wisdom-gnosis,
and fourth initiation. These "completion stage" initiations, although apparently eight, are counted as four: (1) the two vase initiations; (2) the two secret intitiations; (3) the two wisdom-gnosis
initiations together with the fourth initiation of the "higher" set;
and (4) the fourth initiation of the "higher than high" set.

4. The mandala to which a Kalachakra initiate is introduced
must be made of colored sand, or powder.

5. Kalachakra generation stage practices do not include
assumption of a visualized sambhogakaya in order to purify the
intermediate state between death and rebirth. Rather, purification
of the intermediate state is subsumed by the purification of death
and rebirth. These are prefigured by the assumption of the
dharmakaya and nirmanakaya of the deity, at the points in the
sadhana where one reduces oneself to emptiness, then generates
oneself as the deity. One is said to have accomplished the generation stage of the Kalachakra when one can visualize the entire
mandala in a drop the size of a mustard seed at the tip of one's
nose, with such clarity that one can see the whites of the eyes of all
722 deities—and can maintain this visualization with uninterrupted one-pointed concentration for four hours.

6. Kalachakra completion stage practices aim at the production
not of an illusory body, but of a "*mahamudra* of empty form" This
body of empty form differs from an illusory body in that it has as its
material cause not the winds that have been directed into the
central channel, but the mind. In Kalachakra, therefore, both the
dharmakaya (clear light) and the form bodies (empty form) are
based on the mind.

The Kalachakra completion stage consists of six yogas, or
stages, which are generally similar to completion-stage procedures
in other *Anuttara* Yoga tantras and have the same result, buddhahood. The six yogas also have features that differentiate them from
the completion stage practices of other *Anuttara* Yoga tantras, but

we will not detail them here.

FROM INDIAN TO TIBETAN BUDDHISM

Regardless of whether—as a Western-trained scholar might insist—most of the sutra and tantra traditions of Buddhism were evolutionary developments post-dating the Buddha by centuries, or—as a traditionalist might insist—the Buddha taught all the sutras and tantras (although different practices flourished at differ- ent times after his death), it remains the case that Indian Buddhism in the late first millenium A.D.—the time the Kalachakra was re- introduced to India—was a complex tradition, interwoven of Hina- yana, Perfection Vehicle and tantric doctrines and practices.

Buddhism thrived in particular in Bengal, Kashmir, and parts of south India. Its lifeblood, as always, was the monasteries, which in many cases had evolved from simple rainy-season retreats for monks into great universities, such as Nalanda and Vikramashila, where the accumlated lore of centuries was distilled into a course of study that employed lecture, debate, and meditation to familiar- ize students from throughout the Buddhist world with the breadth and depth of the Buddhist tradition, both written and oral. While the tantras were studied and practiced in the monasteries, tantric practice received a great deal of impetus as well from wandering yogis who mingled with the populace, sometimes working won- ders, sometimes singing mysterious songs, but always inspiring dedication to the pursuit of enlightenment.

Indian Buddhism was effectively destroyed by the Turkic Mus- lim invasions of the thirteenth century, but not before it had been transmitted virtually intact to the north, to Tibet. Prior to the seventh century, Tibet had been surrounded by Buddhist coun- tries—with India to the south, China to the east, Khotan to the north, and Kashmir to the west—but had remained a politically disunited collection of feudatories content to practice a shamanic religion known as *Bon*.

In the mid-seventh century, however, a king of Yarlung, Srong btsan sgam po (Songtsen Gampo), united most of the Tibetan nobility under him and turned Tibet into a major military power, sending expeditions to China and Bengal. Spurred by contact with

Buddhist cultures, Srong btsan sgam po introduced a few Buddhist practices into Tibet, took Buddhist wives from China and Nepal, and obtained a script from India on the basis of which Tibetan could at last become a written language.

For much of the following century, Buddhism in Tibet was largely ornamental, used for political and magical leverage by the kings in their struggles with Bonpo nobility. However, a mid-eighth-century monarch, Khri srong lde btsan (Trisong Detsen), was serious enough about Buddhism that he called from India the famous pandit Shantarakshita, who he hoped would found a Tibetan monastic tradition. Shantarakshita encountered opposition from jealous Tibetan nobles and/or gods, so the great tantric wonder-worker, the siddha, Padmasambhava was brought from Oddiyana to eliminate the obstacles. This done, the first Tibetan monastery was founded at bSam yas (Samye).

Chinese Buddhists also were active in Tibet, but their influence declined sharply after their apparent defeat in 792–4 A.D. in a debate with Indian Buddhists. The Indians insisted that the Dharma must be practiced gradually and with full attention to both its method and wisdom sides, and that the Chinese emphasis on the radical "wisdom-only" message of the perfection of wisdom sutras both distorted tradition and encouraged spiritual laziness.

In part through the growth of monasteries, in part through the efforts of wandering tantric yogis, Buddhism continued to grow in popularity, but it still provoked the jealousy of the old Bon po nobility, who, incensed at paying heavy taxes to support Buddhist monasteries, staged a coup d'etat midway through the ninth century. They replaced the Buddhist king Ral pa can (Ralpachen) with the Bonpo gLang dar ma (Langdarma), who instituted a persecution of Buddhism. He was eventually murdered by a Buddhist monk, but not before much of the Buddhist superstructure had been destroyed in Tibet.

The next century-and-a-half were marked by political disunity and the absence of any institutional basis for Buddhism. At the same time, Buddhism continued unofficially to make inroads in Tibet, adapting itself where necessary to Bon po customs while at the same time preserving the fundamental tenor of its doctrines and practices. Generally speaking, Buddhists found a receptive audience in Tibet, because the magical overtones of tantra ac-

corded well with the style of Bon—though in substance or soteriology the two religions were radically different.

Because the Tibetan assimilation of Buddhism during this
period was informal, there was insufficient control over the quality
of thought and practice, and aberrations inevitably sprang up. It
was with an eye to correcting abuses that, early in the eleventh
century, kings of western Tibet invited pandits from India to help
with a new series of translations of Buddhist texts, and nobles in
the Lhasa area managed to revive the monastic tradition.

What followed was a virtual explosion of interest in Buddhism
in Tibet. With the exception of the rNying ma pas, who trace their
traditions back to the eighth-century visit to Tibet of Padmasambhava (or "Guru Rinpoche"), all the schools of Tibetan Buddhism have their roots in the religious ferment of the eleventh
century. The bKa' brgyud (Kargyu) tradition, whose best-known
latter-day representatives have been the *Karmapas*, began when the
translator Mar pa (Marpa) journeyed to India to study with the
great pandit-turned-yogi, Naropa, who had in turn studied with
Tilopa. Such vital practices as the *mahamudra* and the "inner heat"
(*gTum mo*) were conveyed by Mar pa to the yogi-poet Mi la ras pa,
(Milarepa), who, in turn passed them on the sGam po pa (Gam-
popa), the founder of the institutionalized bKa' brgyud tradition.
sGam po pa combined the largely tantric teachings he heard from
Mi la ras pa (Milarepa) with the more "conventional," sutra-ori-
ented approach stressed by teachers in the bKa' gdams (Kadam)
tradition. The bKa' gdams tradition is traced back to Atisha, who
came to Tibet from India in 1042 AD, and spent twelve years
traveling about and teaching.

Atisha neither ignored nor was ignorant of the tantras, but felt
that the Tibetans' greatest need was to establish the foundations of
Buddhist practice. Thus, he emphasized the maintenance of strict
monastic discipline; familiarity with the great Buddhist texts; and
the development of the spirit of renunciation, altruism, and insight
into the nature of reality. Although the bKa gdams tradition would
slowly die out, its emphasis and many of its doctrines would be
taken over in the fourteenth century by Tsong kha pa (Tsong
Khapa), who considered himself a "neo-bKa' dams pa."

The Sa skya (Sakya) tradition derives from the teachings of the
Indian yogi Virupa, which were brought to Tibet by 'Brog mi

(Drogmi). The Sa skya tradition is notable for its combination of an abiding interest in scholarship with a dedication to the practice of both sutra- and tantra-based meditative traditions.

If the eleventh century was the source of many of the doctrinal bases of Tibetan Buddhism, the twelfth century saw the rise of many of its institutions. Nobles in various parts of the country, in search perhaps of religious legitimization—or simply religious power—eagerly assisted the growing community of religious practitioners, in part by funding the establishment of monasteries.

Ironically, though, the power vacuum left by the collapse of the old line of kings in the ninth century was filled not by the *nouveau riche* nobility but by the monasteries, whose sacred associations conferred a unifying power that eventually would be translated into landholdings, financial transactions, and political power.

At about this same time, there also originated the two major methods of monastic succession: succession from uncle to nephew was founded by the Sa skya pas, and succession from reincarnation to reincarnation was instituted by the Karma bKa' brgyd pas.

The thirteenth century was most notable for the ascent to temporal—if not religious—power by the Sa skya pas. When the Mongols threatened to invade Tibet in mid-century, Kun dga'rgyal mtshan (Kunga Gyaltsen), the Sa skya Pandita, went to the Mongol court as an appeaser. He stayed on, and his nephew 'Phags pa (Pagpa) later gained influence with Kublai Khan, who founded the Mongol Yuan dynasty in China. The Khan granted the Sa skya pas hegemony over Tibet, which they held, against growing opposition, for nearly three-quarters of a century.

The Yuan dynasty collapsed early in the fourteenth century, and with it fell the fortunes of the Sa skya pas, who were eclipsed by an upstart noble, Byang chub rgyal mtshan (Jangchub Gyaltsen), associated with the bKa' brgyud monastery at Phag mo gru (Pagmodru), near Lhasa. Byang chub rgyal mtshen ushered in a sort of nationalistic revival, which saw a return to ancient Tibetan festivals, now imbued with Buddhist values; and the discovery by rNying ma pas of *gTer mas* (termas), texts allegedly hidden by Padmasambhava in the eighth century.

Independent Tibetan scholarship, whose first great exemplar was Sa skya Pandita, flourished. kLong chen pa (Longchenpa) systematized the various strands of the rNying ma tradition, giving

particular emphasis to the direct, wisdom-oriented meditation system known as the Great Perfection (*maha ati; rDjzogs chen*). Bu ston
(Buton) commented at length on the *Kalachakra Tantra*, wrote a
history of Buddhism in India and Tibet, and, most importantly,
edited the vast collection of translations from the Indian Buddhist
commentarial tradition, giving us the present form of the *bsTan
'gyur (Tanjur)*, which together with the *bKa' 'gyur (Kanjur)*, (those
texts believed actually expounded by the Buddha,) comprise the
Tibetan Buddhist canon.

bLo bzang grags pa (Lozang Dragpa), better known as Tsong
kha pa, was born in eastern Tibet in 1357. He studied with masters
of all the Tibetan lineages, and went on to forge a new synthesis of
Buddhist learning, as exemplified in his great compendia on the
stages of the sutra and tantra paths. He was tireless in his efforts to
combat doctrinal errors he felt had crept into Tibetan Buddhism
since Atisha. He was particularly concerned with the interpretation of Madhyamika philosophy. He also possessed Atisha's zeal for
monastic reform. He gathered a large following in the Lhasa area
where, in the first two decades of the fifteenth century, he and his
disciples reinstituted the great New Year's festival (*mon lam*), and
founded three great monasteries, dGa' ldan (Ganden), Se ra (Sera),
and 'Bras spungs (Drepung), which were modeled on the monastic
universities of India.

Over the next century-and-a-half, Tsong ka pa's successors,
known as the dGe lugs pas (Gelugpas), were the dominant force in
the Lhasa area, while the region to the west, gTsang, was under the
influence of the Karma bKa' brgyud pas (who also were powerful to
the east, in Khams).

The stalemate began to break in 1578, when bSod nams rgya
mtsho (Sonam Gyatso), an important dGe lugs pa political and
religious figure, gained influence with a Mongol chieftain, who
bestowed upon him the title "Dalai Lama" ("ocean of wisdom").
The title was conferred posthumously on bSod nams rga mtsho's
two previous incarnations, making him the third Dalai Lama.
Newly-invested with temporal legitimacy and possessed of his own
erudition and charisma, the Third Dalai Lama journeyed through
Khams on his way back to Lhasa, winning there many admirers.

The dGe lugs-Mongol connection bore final fruit in the mid-
seventeenth century, when Gushri Khan and his army destroyed the

bases of Karmapa power in both Khams and gTsang and, in effect, presented Tibet to the Fifth Dalai Lama, bLo bzan rgya mtsho (Lozang Gyatso). The Fifth Dalai Lama set about uniting all of Tibet under dGe lugs rule. Some monasteries were forcibly converted, but by and large he was tolerant of other traditions, and established thereby a policy that would be followed by his successors. With their headquarters at the Potala in Lhasa, the Dalai Lamas—recognized as incarnations of the compassionate Buddha Avalokiteshvara—would rule Tibet more or less unchallenged internally for the next three hundred years, until the arrival of Chinese troops in 1950. It was under the rule of the Dalai Lamas that Tibetan Buddhism reached its definitive form, and it is that form—and the Kalachakra's place within it—to which we next turn.

TIBETAN BUDDHISM AND THE KALACHAKRA'S PLACE IN IT

Traditional Tibetan society is, or was—it is difficult to know which tense to use, given the peril in which the tradition finds itself—thoroughly permeated by Buddhism, and was perhaps the most religiously-inclined society still extant in the twentieth century world. From families with their household altars and local ceremonies, to wandering or hermit yogis practicing advanced meditations, to monks studying in the great monasteries, nearly all Tibetans made Buddhism a significant part of their lives.

Most communities could count on the services of a nearby temple or monastery, or at the very least of an itinerant *lama* (a Tibetan term that translates the Sanskrit *guru*, or master, and need not connote an ordained individual.) The services most usually required were the performance of *pujas*, ceremonies of offering and propitiation to deities, who might be expected in return to provide specific desired temporal or spiritual benefits. In its most skeletal form, a puja consists of seven "limbs": prostration, offering, confession, rejoicing in the virtues and happiness of others, requesting the buddhas to continue to turn the Dharma-wheel, entreating them not to enter final nirvana, and dedicating one's merits to the welfare of all sentient beings.

Lamas also often were asked to give discourses on various Buddhist topics, and were expected, too, to perform ceremonies for the dead—whose next rebirth might thereby be improved. Individual lay Buddhists performed various devotions before their household altars, circumambulated local stupas or shrines, and would on occasion undertake pilgrimages to holy spots in Tibet or India, sometimes prostrating the entire way. Seldom far from the lips of Tibetan lay-people, particularly the elderly, was the mantra of Avalokiteshvara: *oM maNi padme huM* which invokes the Buddha's compassion and is said to debar rebirth in the six realms of samsara.

Also an important part of the Tibetan religious scene were lone yogis, who moved between cave and bazaar, sometimes working wonders, and often presenting their insights in the form of popular songs, riddles, and poems. Their progenitors, such beloved figures as Mi la ras pa and 'Brug pa kun legs (Drugpa Kunleg), played a vital role in the popularization of Buddhism in Tibet. Lone yogis continued in modern times to be sources of popular legend and inspiration.

As in India, so in Tibet, the monasteries were the backbone of the continuity of Buddhist tradition. Monasteries ranged from tiny local dgon pas (gompas) to the great universities and colleges of Lhasa. Most monasteries were affiliated with one or the other of the major traditions, and each tradition had its important seats, where the full wealth of the lineage could be transmitted to the most promising students, many of whom were specially recognized reincarnate lamas, or *sPrul skus (tulkus)*.

Among the dGe lugs pas, a young monk's goal often was to be able some day to attend one of the three great universities in Lhasa, dGa' ldan, Se ra, or 'Bras spungs. There, the brightest would enter a twenty-year course of study that led to the conferral of the *dGe bshes (geshe)* degree, signifying mastery of all the most important branches of Buddhist learning. *dGe bshes* candidates were expected to know such arts as poetry, painting, grammar, and medicine, but primarily they were responsible for thoroughly learning the great Buddhist texts.

The course of study included (1) ethics and monastic discipline, based on the various recensions of the Vinaya; (2) logic and epistemology, based on the *Pramanavarttika* of Dharmakirti; (3) the Perfection of Wisdom sutras and their implicit path-system, based on the *Abhisamayalamkara* of Maitreya; (4) Madhyamika, based on the

Madhyamakakarikas of Nagarjuna and the *Madhyamakavatara* of Chandrakirti; and (5) *abhidharma* discussions of cosmology, meta-physics, and the phenomenology of mind, based on the *Abhidhar-makosha* of Vasubandhu and the *Abhidharmasamuccaya* of Asanga. These ancient texts often were studied with the aid of Tibetan-written textbooks called *yig chas*, and the insights contained in them were refined by constant testing and debate.

The dGe lugs pas also had two important colleges that special-ized in the tantras, rGyud stod (Gyuto) and rGyud med (Gyume). There, one might learn the proper performance of tantric rituals, the art of making mandalas and offering-substances and—most importantly—how properly to practice the sadhanas of the various tantric deities. All four classes of tantra have been preserved and transmitted by Tibetan traditon, although the lowest and highest, *Kriya* and *Anuttara* Yoga, are the most commonly practiced.

Students at rGyud stod and rGyud med develop expertise in the systems of Guhyasamaja, Chakrasamvara, and Yamantaka (or Vajra-bhairava), but they do not study the Kalachakra system.

Indeed, the Kalachakra plays a vital but ambiguous role in Tibetan Buddhism. On the one hand, it is conceded by most tradi-tions to be the very pinnacle of the Buddha's teaching. Its eschatol-ogy—with its discussion of the role of the land of Shambhala in a future armageddon and revival of the Dharma—is widely accepted, and considered to make it especially important to the present "degenerate" era. Therfore, the Kalachakra has become the one *Anuttara* Yoga tantra whose initiations are given to large public gatherings, most notably by the Dalai Lama.

At the same time, the Kalachakra is universally conceded to be the most complex and recondite of all Buddhist teachings, and it is studied in detail by very few. Each tradition has a few masters who are expert in it. The Panchen and Dalai Lamas traditionally have studied and transmitted it, and its practices are the specialty of the small monastic college most closely associated with the Dalai Lamas, rNam rgyal (Namgyal).

However arcane the Kalachakra and other tantric systems may be, they nonetheless are an integral part of the organism that is Tibetan Buddhism, where the higher practices invariably are based on the lower, the lower invariably point toward the higher, and the beginning and end of the path are mutually influential. All

Tibetan practices are supposed to arise out of the Mahayana spirit, and to maintain what Tsong kha pa called the "three principal aspects of the path to enlightenment": (1) a renunciation of the suffering of samsara and its cause, coupled with a strong desire to attain liberation; (2) *bodhicitta*, or the aspiration to attain enlightenment for the sake of aiding all sentient beings, and (3) realization—first through reason and then directly—of the ultimate nature of all phenomena, that is, emptiness—the realization of which is the basis for the eradication of the defilements that perpetuate one's samsaric suffering.

Tibetan Buddhism, then, is a *lam rim* or unified path with many stages, a gradual ascent from the most basic questions to the most thoroughgoing answers and achievements, a single tradition in which the smile of Shakyamuni and the smile of Kalachakra are united. The gradual unfolding of the path as one moves from fundamental devotional and ethical practices to the subtle processes of tantra is beautifully expressed in the verses—attributed to the First Panchen Lama, bLo bzang chos kyi rgyal mtshan (Lozang Chokyi Gyaltsen)—known as "(The Prayer) to Become the Foundation of Good Qualities" (*Yon tan gZir gyur ma*):

Seeing that the kind, holy (guru) is the foundation of good qualities, and that proper reliance is the root of the path, I ask blessing to rely on (the guru) with great respect (born) of constant effort.

Knowing the rarity and great significance of this (human body) that is the wonderful basis of an opportunity obtained just once, I ask blessing to generate uninterruptedly, all the day and night, the mind that takes up what is essential (to obtaining buddhahood).

Remembering that death will swiftly destroy my wavering body and life, which are like bubbles on a stream, and gaining firm recognition that the effects of my white and black actions will follow me after death like a body's shadow, I ask blessing to take care always to avoid even the subtlest fault and to accomplish all that is virtuous.

Aware of the disadvantages of worldly goods—(for they are) unsatisfying when consumed, untrustworthy, and the door to all suffering—I ask blessing to generate the great striving for the bliss of liberation.

I ask blessing to take as my essential practice the guidelines for individual liberation (Pratimoksha vows), which are the root of the Dharma, (and to do so) with the great care of mindfulness and introspection induced by that pure thought (renouncing samsara and striving for liberation).

Seeing that, just as I have fallen into the ocean of samsara, so too have all transmigrating beings, who have been my mothers, I ask blessing to develop the supreme thought of enlightenment, which takes on the burden of liberating transmigrating beings.

Seeing that if I generate just the thought (of enlightenment), and do not cultivate the three types of (bodhisattva) morality, I will not attain enlightenment, I ask blessing to train assiduously in the vows of the Conqueror's (children) (bodhisattvas).

I ask blessing to generate quickly in my mindstream the union of calm and insight, through pacifying (a mind) that strays toward false objects, and investigating properly the ultimate object (emptiness).

When I have become a (suitable spiritual) vessel, trained in the common (Perfection Vehicle) path, I ask blessing happily to enter the highest of all vehicles, the Vajrayana, the holy crossing-boat for fortunate beings.

Gaining then genuine certainty (that I must guard) the pure (tantric) vows that are the foundation of accomplishing (mundane and trans-mundane) attainments, I ask blessing to guard (those vows) at the risk of my life.

Understanding then the essentials of the (generation and completion) stages that are the heart of the (four) classes of tantra, I ask blessing to practice according to the teachings of the holy ones, without neglecting to practice yoga in four sessions (daily).

May virtuous (teachers) who show the good path, and friends who practice it properly, have long life. I ask blessing to pacify swiftly outer and inner hindrances.

In all my lives, may I never be apart from the perfect master, and may I enjoy the splendor of the Dharma. Having perfected the good qualities of the (ten bodhisattva) stages and the (five) paths, may I quickly attain the rank of Vajradhara.

REFERENCES AND FURTHER READING

Section 1

For historians' views of the history of Buddhism, cf. e.g., A.K. Warder, *Indian Buddhism*, 2nd ed. (Delhi: Motilal Banarsidass, 1970); Richard Robinson and Willard Johnson, *The Buddhist Religion: A Historical Introduction*, 3rd ed. (Belmont, CA: Wadsworth, 1982); and Charles S. Prebish, ed., *Buddhism: A Modern Perspective* (University Park: The Pennsylvania State University Press, 1975).

For traditional histories, cf., e.g., F.D. Lessing and A. Wayman, tr., *Introduction to the Buddhist Tantric Systems* (Delhi: Motilal Banarsidass, 1978), chapters two and three; Bu ston, *Jewelry of Scripture*, tr. E. Obermiller (Heidelberg, 1931); and Taranatha, *History of Buddhism in India*, tr. Lama Chimpa and Alaka Chattopadhyaya (Simla: Indian Institute of Advanced Study, 1970).

Section 2

For historians' versions of the Buddha's life, cf. e.g., E.J. Thomas, *The Life of the Buddha as Legend and History* (Boston: Routledge and Kegan Paul, 1975) and Alfred Foucher, *The Life of the Buddha According to the Ancient Texts and Monuments of India* (Middletown, CT: Wesleyan University Press, 1963).

Traditional biographies include Ashvaghosha, *The Buddhacarita or Acts of the Buddha*, tr. E.H. Johnston (Delhi: Motilal Banarsidass, 1972) and the *Lalitavistara*, which has been translated into English and published recently by Dharma Press, Emeryville, California.

For Theravada versions of the Buddha's life, cf., e.g., Bhikkhu Nanamoli, *The Life of the Buddha* (Kandy, Sri Lanka, Buddhist Publication Society, 1972) and David and Indrani Kalupahana, *The Way of Siddhartha: A Life of the Buddha* (Boulder: Shambhala, 1982).

Tibetan versions of the Buddha's life may be found in Lessing and Wayman, Bu ston and Taranatha, *op. cit.* (section 1).

Section 3

Some traditional outlines of the Buddhist world-view include Tenzin Gyatso (Dalai Lama XIV), *The Opening of the Wisdom Eye*, tr. Bhikkhu Khantipalo *et. al.* (Wheaton, IL: Theosophical Publishing House); sGam po pa, *The Jewel Ornament of Liberation*, tr. H.V. Guenther (Berkeley: Shambhala, 1971); Geshe Ngagwang Dhargyey, *Tibetan Tradition of Mental Development* (Dharamsala: Library of Tibetan Works and Archives, 1974); Shantarakshita, *The Tattvasamgraha of Shantarakshita, with the Commentary of Kamalashila*, tr. Ganganatha Jha, 2 vols. (Baroda: Oriental Institute, 1937, 1939); Geshe Lhundub Sopa and Jeffery Hopkins, *Practice and Theory of Tibetan Buddhism* (New York: Grove Press, 1976); Asanga, *Le Compendium du Super-Doctrine: L'Abhidharmasamuccaya d'Asanga*, tr. Walpola Rahula (Paris: École Francaise d'Extrême-Orient, 1971; and Vasubadhu, *L'Abhidharmakosha de Vasubandhu*, tr. Louis de la Vallée Poussin, 6 vols. (Paris: Paul Geuthner, 1923–31).

Section 4

The source of the theory of the three turnings of the Dharma-wheel is the *Sam-dhinirmocana Sutra*, which has been translated by Etienne Lamotte in *Samdhinirmo-cana Sutra: Explication des Mysteres* (Louvain: Universite de Louvain, 1935). Lessing and Wayman, Bu ston, Taranatha and Sopa and Hopkins all contain accounts of the three turnings.

The main content of the first turning is, of course, reflected in the Pali canon, which has been translated *in toto* by the Pali Text Society, London; a good basic account of the Theravadin tradition is Walpola Rahula, *What the Buddha Taught* (New York: Grove Press, 1974), while a superb philosophical discussion is K.N. Jayatilleke, *Early Buddhist Theory of Knowledge* (Delhi: Motilal Banarsidass, 1980). The classic exposition of the Vaibhashika/Sarvastivadin position is Vasubandhu's *Abhidharmakosha* (cf. section 3); works exposing the Sautrantika position include Theodore Stcherbatsky, *Buddhist Logic*, 2 vols. (New York: Dover, 1962) and Satkari Mookerjee, *The Buddhist Doctrine of the Universal Flux* (Delhi: Motilal Banarsidass, 1980). Expositions of the views of the Hinayana schools also may be found in Sopa and Hopkins, *op. cit.*, and Andre Bareau, *Les Sectes Bouddhiques du Petit Vehicule* (Paris: École Française d'Extrême Orient, 1955).

The second turning is represented in the sutra traditon by, e.g., Edward Conze, *The Perfection of Wisdom in Eight Thousand Lines and Its Verse Summary* (Bolinas, CA: Four Seasons Foundation, 1973); Edward Conze, *Buddhist Wisdom Books: The Diamond Sutra and the Heart Sutra* (New York: Harper & Row, 1972); Robert A.F. Thurman, tr., *The Holy Teaching of Vimalakirti* (University Park, PA: Pennsylvania State University Press, 1976); D.T. Suzuki, tr., *The Lankavatara Sutra* (London: Routledge and Kegan Paul, 1973); and Alex and Hideko Wayman, *The Lion's Roar of Queen Srimala: A Buddhist Scripture on the Tathagatagarbha Theory* (New York: Columbia University Press, 1974). On Madhyamika, the philosophical school associated with the second turning, cf., e.g., Frederick Streng, *Emptiness: A Study in Religious Meaning* (Nashville: Abingdon Press, 1967), Dalai Lama XIV, *The Buddhism of Tibet and the Key to the Middle Way* (London: George Allen & Unwin, 1975); Jeffrey Hopkins, *Meditation on Emptiness* (London: Wisdom Publications, 1984); and D. Seyfort Ruegg, *The Literature of the Madhyamika School of Philosophy in India* (Wiesbaden: Harrassowitz, 1981). On tathagatagarbha, cf. Ruegg's *La Theorie du Tathagata-garbah et du Gotra* (Paris: École Française d'Extrême-Orient, 1969). The chief sutra of the third turning is the *Samdhinirmocana Sutra* (cf. above). For expositions of Yogachara, cf., e.g., Sylvain Levi, tr., *Mahayanasutralamkara* (Paris: Bibliotheque de l'École des Hautes Etudes, 1907, 1911); Asanga, *La Somme du Grand Vehicule d'Asanga (Mahayanasamgraha)*, tr. Etienne Lamotte, 2 vols. (Louvain: Bureaux du Museon, 1938, 1939); Louis de la Vallée Poussin, *Le Siddhi de Hsuan-tsang*, 3 vols. (Paris: Paul Geuthner, 1928–48); and Stephan Anacker, *Seven Works of Vasubandhu* (Delhi: Motilal Banarsidass, 1984).

Section 5

The classic exposition of the Theravadin path-system is Buddhaghosa, *The Path of Purification (Visuddhimagga)*, tr. Bhikkhu Nanamoli, 2 vols. (Berkeley: Shambhala, 1976).

The classic exposition of the path-systems adhered to by the Hinayana schools is Vasubandhu's *Abhidharmakosha*.

The source of most later Mahayana path-theory is the *Abhisamayalamkara*, tr. Edward Conze (Roma: Instituto Italiano per itl Medio ed Estremo Oriente, 1954).

General accounts of the various path systems may be found in Sopa and Hopkins, *op. cit.*; Prebish, *op. cit.* (cf. section 1), chapters 26–27); Har Dayal, *The Bodhisattva Doctrine in Buddhist Sanskrit Literature* (Delhi: Motilal Banarsidass, 1975); Mark Tatz and Jody Kent, *Rebirth: The Tibetan Game of Liberation* (New York: Anchor, 1977); Geshe Kelsang Gyatso, *Meaningful to Behold: View, Meditation, and Action in Mahayana Buddhism* (Ulverston, England: Wisdom Publications, 1980); and E. Obermiller, *Analysis of the Abhisamayalamkara*, 2 vols. (London: Luzac & Co., 1933, 1936).

On the *ekayana*, cf. Ruegg, *La Theorie du Tathagatagarbha*, and the classic exposition of the theory in H. Kern, tr., *Saddharmapundarika Sutra or the Lotus of the True Law* (New York: Dover, 1963).

Section 6

For reliable general accounts of tantra, cf. e.g., Lessing and Wayman, *op. cit.*; John Blofeld, *The Tantric Mysticism of Tibet* (New York: Dutton, 1970); Tsong kha pa, *Tantra in Tibet*, tr. Jeffrey Hopkins (Boston: George Allen & Unwin, 1977); Stephan Beyer, *The Cult of Tara* (Berkeley: University of California Press, 1973); Agehananda Bharati, *The Tantric Tradition* (New York: Samuel Weiser, 1975); and Lama Anagarika Govinda, *Foundations of Tibetan Mysticism* (New York: Samuel Weiser, 1977).

On guru devotion, cf., e.g., Ashvaghosa, *Fifty Verses on Guru Devotion* (Dharamsala: Library of Tibetan Works and Archives, 1974); Lobsang P. Lhalungpa, tr., *The Life of Milarepa* (New York: Dutton, 1977); and Herbert V. Guenther, tr., *The Life and Teaching of Naropa* (New York: Oxford University Press, 1963).

On tantric iconography and symbolism, cf., e.g., Detlef Ingo Lauf, *Tibetan Sacred Art* (Berkeley: Shambhala, 1976); Alice Getty, *The Gods of Northern Buddhism* (Rutland, VT: Charles Tuttle, 1977); Loden Sherap Dagyab, *Tibetan Religious Art*, 2 vols. (Wiesbaden: Harrassowitz, 1977); Govinda, *op. cit.*; and A. Wayman, *The Buddhist Tantras: Light on Indo-Tibetan Esotericism* (New York: Samuel Weiser, 1973).

On the subtle body, cf. Govinda, *op.cit.*; Mircea Eliade, *Yoga: Immortality and Freedom* (Princeton: Princeton University Press, 1969); and Geshe Kelsang Gyatso, *Clear Light of Bliss: Mahamudra in Vajrayana Buddhism* (London: Wisdom Publications, 1982).

On initiations, cf. Lessing and Wayman, *op. cit.*, chapters eight and nine; C.A. Muses, ed., *Esoteric Teachings of the Tibetan Tantra*, tr. Chang Chen Chi (New York: Samuel Weiser, 1982); and *Kalachakra Initiation: Madison, 1981* (Madison, WI: Deer Park, 1981).

On sadhana, cf., e.g., Blofeld, *op. cit.*; Beyer, *op. cit.*; Janice Dean Willis, *The Diamond Light: An Introduction to Tibetan Buddhist Meditations* (New York: Simon & Schuster, 1972); Benoytosh Bhattacharyya, *Sadhanamala* (Baroda: Gaekwad's Oriental Series, no 41, 1928)l and Bhattacharyya's *Indian Buddhist Iconography* (London: Oxford University Press, 1924).

An excellent annotated bibliography of works about tantra is found in David Reigle, *The Books of Kiu-Te or the Tibetan Buddhist Tantras* (San Diego: Wizards Bookshelf, 1983).

Section 7

On the rNying ma pa way of arranging the tantras, cf. Herbert V. Guenther, *Buddhist Philosophy in Theory and Practice* (Berkeley: Shambhala, 1971); on the Sar ma pa arrangement accepted by the Sa skya pas, bKa gyu pas and dGe lug pas, cf. Lessing and Wayman, *op. cit.*; and Tsong kha pa, *op. cit.*

On *Kriya* and *Charya* tantra cf. Lessing and Wayman, chapters four and five; and Tsong kha pa, *The Yoga of Tibet*, tr. Jeffrey Hopkins (London: George Allen & Unwin, 1981).

On Yoga tantra, cf. Lessing and Wayman, chapter six. Cf. also Minoru Kiyota, *Shingon Buddhism: Theory and Practice* (Los Angeles: Buddhist Books International, 1978), which is an account of Yoga tantra as practiced in the Japanese Buddhist tradition.

More specific bibliographical information in Reigle, *op. cit.*

Section 8.

On *Anuttara* Yoga tantra in general, cf. Lessing and Wayman, chapter seven; Beyer, *op. cit.*; and Alex Wayman, *Yoga of the Guhyasamaja Tantra: The Arcane Lore of the Forty Verses* (New York: Samuel Weiser, 1980).

Partial or complete translations of *Anuttara* Yoga tantras include David Snell-grove, tr., *The Hevajra Tantra*, 2 vols. (London: Oxford University Press, 1959); Shinichi Tsuda, *The Samvarodaya Tantra, selected chapters* (Tokyo: The Hokuseido Press, 1974). Of the *Guhyasamaja Tantra*, chapter 1 has been translated in Giuseppe Tucci, *Theory and Practice of the Mandala* (New York: Samuel Weiser, 1969); chapters 6 and 12 in Wayman, *Yoga of the Guhyasamaja*; and chapter 7 in Edward Conze, *Buddhist Texts Through the Ages* (New York: Harper & Row, 1954).

Publicly available *Anuttara* Yoga tantra generation-stage sadhanas include a Chakrasamvara sadhana in Stephan Beyer, *The Buddhist Experience: Sources and Interpretations* (Belmont, CA: Dickenson, 1974); and those contained in Bhatta-charyya, *op. cit.*

Anuttara Yoga tantra completion-stage practices are discussed in, e.g., Gyatso, *Clear Light of Bliss*; Lati Rinbochay and Jeffrey Hopkins, *Death, Intermediate State and Rebirth in Tibetan Buddhism* (Valois, NY: Gabriel/Snow Lion, 1979); Guenther, *The Life and Teaching of Naropa*; Panchen Lama I, *The Great Seal of Voidness: The Root Text for the Gelug-Kagyu Tradition of Mahamudra*, tr. Geshe Ngagwang Dhargyey *et al.* (Dharamsala: Library of Tibetan Works and Archives, 1975); W.Y. Evans-Wentz, *Tibetan Yoga and Secret Doctrines* (New York: Oxford University Press, 1967); and Long chen rab jam pa, *An Introduction to Dzog Chen: The Four-Themed Precious Gar-land*, tr. A. Berzin (Dharamsala: Library of Tibetan Works and Archives, 1975).

Section 9

On the Kalachakra in general, cf. Edwin Bernbaum, *The Way to Shambhala* (Garden City, NY: Anchor, 1980); Helmut Goffmann, "Buddha's Preaching of the *Kalacakra Tantra* at the Stupa of Dhanyakataka" in *German Scholars on India*, vol. I (Varanasi, 1973), pp. 136–40; Helmut Hoffmann, "Kalachakra Studies I: Manichaeism, Chris-tianity and Islam in the *Kalachakra Tantra* in *Central Asiatic Journal* 13 (1969), pp.

52–73 (addenda and corrigenda published in CAJ 15 (1971–72), pp. 298–301; Gar je K'am trul Rinpoche, "A Geography and History of Shambhala," tr. Sharpa Tulku and A. Berzin, in *The Tibet Journal* 3:3 (1978); A. Csoma de Koros, "Note on the Origin of the Kala Cakra and Adi Buddha Systems," *Journal of the Asiatic Society of Bengal* 2 (1833), pp. 57–59; Georges de Roerich, "Studies in the Kalacakra" in *Urusvati Journal* 2 (1932), pp. 11–22; Roerich, tr., *The Blue Annals* (Delhi: Motilal Banarsidass, 1976, pp. 753 -838; His Holiness the 14th Dalai Lama, *Concerning the Kalacakra Initiation in America* (Madison, WI: Deer Park, 1981; Raghu Vira and Lokesh Chandra, eds., *Kalacakra Tantra and Other Texts,* part I (Delhi: Satapitaka Series, 69, 1966), pp. 5–20; and *Kalacakra Initiation, op.cit.*

On the Kalachakra initiation, cf. *Kalachakra Initiation, op. cit.*; Jeffrey Hopkins, *Kalachakra Tantra* (London: Wisdom Publications, 1985); and Mario E. Carelli, *Shekodeshatika of Nadapada (Naropa): Being a Commentary of the Shekkodesha Section of the Kalachakra Tantra* (Baroda: Gaekwad's Oriental Series, XC, 1941), pp. 5–35.

On the Kalachakra sadhana, cf. *Kalachakra Initiation, op. cit.*

On the completion stage of Kalachakra, cf. Gendun Drub, the First Dalai Lama, *Bridging the Sutras and Tantras,* tr. Glenn H. Mullin (Ithaca, NY: Gabriel/Snow Lion, 1982), pp.115–156.

Section 10

The best all-purpose accounts of Tibetan culture, history and religion are: David Snellgrove and Hugh Richardson, *A Cultural History of Tibet* (New York: Prager, 1968); R.A. Stein, *Tibetan Civilization,* tr. J. Driver (Stanford: Stanford University Press, 1972) and Giuseppe Tucci, *The Religions of Tibet,* tr. Walter Samuel (Berkeley: University of California Press, 1980). A classic, but difficult to obtain, is Tucci's *Tibetan Painted Scrolls,* 3 vols. (Roma: Librerio dello Stato, 1949).

On Nyingmapa, cf., e.g., Longchenpa, *Kindly Bent to Ease Us,* tr. H.V. Guenther, 3 vols. (Emeryville, CA: Dharma Publishing, 1975) Eva Dhargyey, *The Rise of Esoteric Buddhism in Tibet* (Delhi: Motilal Banarsidass, 1977); Yeshe Tsogyal, *The Life and Liberation of Padmasambhava,* 2 vols. (Emeryville, CA: Dharma Publishing, 1980); and Chogyam Trungpa and Francesca Freemantle, tr., *The Tibetan Book of the Dead: The Great Liberation Through Hearing in the Bardo* (Boulder: Shambhala, 1978)

On Kargupa, cf., e.g., sGam po pa, *op. cit.* (cf. section 3); Lhalungpa, *op. cit.* (cf. section 6); Milarepa, *The Hundred Thousand Songs of Milarepa,* tr. Garma C.C. Chang, 2 vols. (Boulder: Shambhala, 1979); Nalanda Translation Committee, *The Life of Marpa the Translator* (Boulder: Shambhala, 1983); Nalanda Translation Committee, *The Rain of Wisdom* (Boulder: Shambhala, 1980); Nik Douglas and Meryl White, *Karmapa: The Black Hat Lama of Tibet* (London: Luzac, 1976); and Jamgon Kongtrul, *The Torch of Certainty,* tr. Judith Hanson (Boulder: Shambhala, 1977).

On Gelugpa, cf., e.g., Dalai Lama VII, *Songs of Spiritual Change,* tr. Glenn H. Mullin (Ithaca, NY: Gabriel/Snow Lion, 1982); Gendun Drub, *op. cit.* (cf. section 9); Geshe Wangyal, *The Door of Liberation* (New York: Maurice Girodias, 1973); Robert A.F. Thurman, *The Life and Teachings of Tsong Khapa* (Dharamsala: Library of Tibetan Works and Archives, 1982); Thurman, *Tsong Khapa's Speech of Gold in the Essence of True Eloquence* (Princeton: Princeton University Press, 1984); Hopkins, *Meditation on Emptiness* (cf. section 4); Gyatso, *Clear Light of Bliss*; Geshe Rabten, *The Life and Teaching of Geshe Rabten: A Tibetan Lama's Search for Truth,* tr. B. Alan Wallace

(Boston: Allen & Unwin, 1980); Dhargyey, *Tibetan Tradition of Mental Development* (cf. section 3); and Geshe Rabten, *The Essential Nectar* (London: Wisdom Publications, 1984).

Section 11

Cf. above references. For alternative translations of the final prayer here, cf. *The Bodhicitta Vows and Lam Rim Puja* (Dharamsala: Library of Tibetan Works and Archives, 1974); and Wangyal, *op. cit.*, pp. 55-57.

These references barely skim the surface of what is available on Buddhism. For further references, readers are referred to, e.g., Kenneth K. Inada, *Guide to Buddhist Philosophy* (Boston: G.K. Hall, 1981); Frank E. Reynolds, *Guide to Buddhist Religion* (Boston: G.K. Hall, 1981); Edward Conze, *Buddhist Scriptures: A Bibliography* (New York: Garland, 1982); Karl Potter, *Bibliography of Indian Philosophy* (Delhi: Motilal Banarsidass, 1974); A.K. Warder, *Indian Buddhism* (cf. section 1); and Robinson and Johnson, *The Buddhist Religion* (cf. section 1).

THE WHEEL OF TIME

A Brief History of the Kalachakra

JOHN R. NEWMAN

INTRODUCTION

The history and mythology of the Kalachakra, the "Wheel of Time," is a fascinating subject. The bodhisattvas and vajracharyas responsible for the transmission of this unique Vajrayana Buddhist tradition are a colorful group, and their deeds are often astonishing. In this essay, I will describe the history of the Kalachakra from its origin to the present, and then continue with what is forecast for the future. I hope that this brief history will increase the reader's appreciation of the Wheel of Time.

Myth and history meet and mingle in the Kalachakra, and many of the elements in this mixture are amenable to more than one interpretation. In other words, Buddhist proponents of the Kalachakra may accept a given portion of the following account as representing both an actual historical event occurring in the world, and as an allegory symbolizing a yogic process occuring within the practitioner of the Kalachakra. The symbolic nature of the Kalachakra's history is due to a special correspondence set up between the historical drama occurring in the macrocosm of world history, and the spiritual drama unfolding in the microcosm of a person's religious transformation. This correspondence is one of the features that distinguishes the Kalachakra from other Buddhist tantric systems, and many pitfalls can be avoided by keeping in mind the multivalent character of the mythopoetic elements in the history of the Kalachakra.

The history of the Kalachakra is contained in a variety of written and oral sources: late-classical Buddhist Sanskrit texts and their Tibetan translations, subsequent Tibetan commentarial and historical exegesis, and the living Tibetan oral tradition. Much of this essay is based on Sanskrit texts that, with their Tibetan translations, are the common property of all the different Tibetan Kalachakra traditions. However, the Sanskrit sources are often open to varying interpretations. Tibetan scholars who have concerned themselves with this topic have produced a voluminous literature that is full of controversies about various important details in the history of the Kalachakra tradition.

Entering into these controversies is an enterprise that would take us far beyond the scope of the present study. Moreover, I will not engage in a critical evaluation of the source materials. Rather, I will present the history of the Kalachakra as it is recounted by the dGe lug pa (Gelugpa) school of Tibetan Buddhism, thus allowing the Buddhists to present their own version of the evolution of the Kalachakra tradition.

THE TEACHING OF THE *PARAMADIBUDDHA* (THE KALACHAKRA *MULATANTRA*)[1]

His Holiness Tenzin Gyatso, the 14th Dalai Lama, has written:

> Because these teachings were given by mystical manifestations of the Buddha to those in a mystical state of purified karma and perception, it does not matter much whether or not any specific tantra in question was expounded during the life of the historical Buddha. Yet, in fact the *Root Tantra* (*Mulatantra*) of Kalachakra was set forth by the Buddha during his life.[2]

The *Paramadibuddha*, the original textual redaction of the Kala-

chakra system, was taught by the Buddha one year after his enlightenment. It was the full moon of *Caitra* (March–April), the first
month of the year in the Kalachakra reckoning. It was the time for
the conquest of Mara called "Victorious Over the Three Worlds."
To the front or east was the full moon; to the back or west was the
sun; to the left or north, was Rahu, the "head of the dragon," or
ascending node of the moon; to the right or south, was Kalagni, the
"tail of the dragon," or descending node of the moon. And, at this
same time, while he taught the Kalachakra at Dhanyakataka, the
Buddha was dwelling on Vulture Heap, Grdhrakuta, near Rajgir in
present-day Bihar, with a vast entourage of bodhisattvas, and was
teaching them the Perfection of Wisdom.

The Buddha taught the Kalachakra inside of the stupa known
as Shri Dhanyakataka.[3] This stupa was the site of a great Vajrayana
concourse at which the Buddha taught not only the system of the
Kalachakra tantra, but also that of the Vajrabhairava or Yamantaka,
the Heruka or Chakrasamvara, and all the other tantric systems as
well. Although these systems first became widely known in India
through their Sanskrit redactions, the *Paramadibuddha* states that
they were in fact originally taught in various languages, in accordance with the dispositions of various sentient beings.

Futhermore, the Vajrayana, or Mantrayana, teachings did not
originate with the Shakyamuni, the historical Buddha; he merely
represented doctrines that had been taught in a previous eon by
Dipamkara Buddha, the buddha who had predicted Shakyamuni's
enlightenment.

The Buddha was dwelling inside the Shri Dhanyakataka stupa,
in a cavern miraculously expanded to gigantic proportions. He
emitted two mandalas. Below was the mandala, the "Sphere of
Phenomena," of a form of Manjushri, called Dharmadhatuvagis-
vara, the Lord of Speech; above was the splendid mandala of the
asterisms.

In the form of Kalachakra, the Buddha stood on the vajra lion
throne in the middle of the great mandala of the "Sphere of Vajra"
(vajradhatu) the abode of great bliss. He was absorbed in the Paramadibuddha (Kalachakra) samadhi. Inside the mandala he was
encircled by a host of buddhas, bodhisattvas, wrathful kings, gods,
nagas, and male and female deities. Outside the mandala were the
disciples. These included the ninety-six satraps of Shambhala,

headed by the requestor of the tantra, King Suchandra of Shambhala, an emanation of Vajrapani.

The entire three realms (the desire, form, and formless realms) saluted the feet of the Buddha, and bodhisattvas, demons, and gods made copious offerings of divine flowers, food, music, and so forth. Representing the entire assembly, Suchandra miraculously entered the dharmadhatu mandala, circumambulated the Teacher, and offered jeweled flowers at his feet. He saluted the Buddha again and again, and sat down before him. With folded hands, Suchandra requested initiation into, and instruction on, the Kalachakra tantra. The Buddha was pleased by Suchandra's request, and he bestowed the full eleven Kalachakra initiations (the ten worldly initiations and the eleventh, transcendental initiation) on everyone assembled there. He taught the twelve thousand verse *Paramadibuddha* in five chapters or investigations: cosmos, soul, initiation, practice, and gnosis. He then predicted the careers of the subsequent kings of Shambhala, the enlightenment of the gods and demons, and the attainment of the noble path by the sentient beings dwelling in the 960 million villages in the lands of Shambhala, and so forth. Suchandra wrote down the *Paramadibuddha* in a volume and, accompanied by his satraps, returned to Shambhala.

SHAMBHALA[4]

As the circumstances of the first teaching of the Kalachakra indicate, this Vajrayana system is closely connected to the land of Shambhala. Shambhala lies north of India and the Himalayas. It is north of the Sita River (the Tarim River in Eastern Turkistan). It is a land of tantric adepts, and its geography reflects this. Shambhala is shaped like a giant lotus having eight petals. The outer perimeter of the entire lotus is formed by a circle of great snow mountains, as is the perimeter of the pericarp that makes up the central third of the country. The interstices of the lotus petals are formed by rivers and snow mountains, and the entire land is covered with beautiful lakes, ponds, meadows, forests, and groves.

The central pericarp of Shambhala is elevated a bit above the surrounding lotus petals, and on it stands the capital of Shambhala, Kalapa. Kalapa is twelve leagues in breadth, and its palaces are made of gold, silver, turquoise, coral, pearl, emerald, moon-crystal, and other precious stones. Kalapa blazes with such a luster that the full moon is a mere pale disc overhead. The light given off by the mirrors on the outside of the palaces is so bright that night cannot be distinguished from day. The thrones inside the palaces are made from the finest beaten gold, and from the gold of the Jambu River. In front of the thrones are crystal looking-glasses that allow one to see far into the distance. On the ceilings are special circular crystal skylights that allow one to observe the palaces, gods, and parks of the sun, moon, and stars, as well as the rotating celestial spheres, and even the zodiac, all as though they were right in front of one. Surrounding the thrones in the palaces are lattice-work screens made of sandalwood that exude fragrances that scent the air for miles. The couches and cushions are all made of the finest, most precious fabrics. In brief, each building in Kalapa is worth many huge ships piled full of gold.

North of Kalapa there are wooded, craggy, crystalline peaks. On the faces of the peaks are very tall designs depicting the buddhas and gods. When seen from a distance, the depictions are very clear, but when viewed up close, they become indistinct. There are one hundred thousand of these images, ten thousand of each of the ten bodhisattvas: Bhadrapala, Merusikharadhara, Kshitigarbha, Man-jushri, Avalokitahalahala, Arya Tara, Guhyakadhipati Vajrapani, Devi Kesini, Paramarthasamudgata, and Maitreya.

South of the village of Kalapa there is a sandalwood pleasure grove. It is twelve leagues in breadth, the same as the village of Kalapa. East of the grove is a miniature Manasa lake, twelve leagues in breadth. To the west is a white lotus lake having the same measure. Humans, gods, and nagas enjoy themselves on the lakes in boats made of jewels.

The sandalwood pleasure grove is between the two lakes, and in the middle of the grove is the mandala circle of Bhagavan (Lord) Kalachakra that was made by King Suchandra. The mandala consists of male and female deities, and it is fashioned from the five precious materials: gold, silver, turquoise, coral, and pearl. This mandala is three-dimensional, square, and four hundred cubits in breadth.

To the outside is the body mandala. It is square, has four entrances, four portals, and is adorned with eight charnel grounds.

It is enclosed by five fences, and outside it is adorned with four discs of earth, water, fire, and wind, and then with a row of vajras. The diameter of the vajra row is eight hundred cubits.

The speech mandala is in the middle of the body mandala; it is square, and half the measure of the body mandala. It has four entrances and is adorned with four portals. It is enclosed by five fences.

The mind mandala is half the size of the speech mandala. It is square, has four entrances and is adorned with four portals. It is enclosed by three fences.

The gnosis circle is half the size of the mind mandala. It is beautified by sixteen pillars. The eight-petaled lotus is half the size of the gnosis circle. One-third of the lotus is its pericarp.

Thus, the body, speech, and mind mandalas are endowed with all the prescribed characteristics. They are furnished with strings and half-strings of pearls. They possess jeweled tapestries, daises, and *bakuli* trees. They are illuminated by mirrors, half-moons, and bells. This mandala was erected by King Suchandra, but there are also many other marvelous mandalas in the grove that were erected by the kings that followed him.

The Kalki (the lineage king) of Shambhala binds his hairlocks on top of his head; he wears a sacred headdress made out of dyed lion's hair and a crown marked with the symbols of the five buddha families. He wears the costume of a universal emperor (*chakravartiraja*), and fortunate people are able to obtain the good path just by seeing or touching him. The Kalki's emblematic earrings, and the bracelets on his arms and legs are made of the gold from the Jambu River. The light from his ornaments mixes with the light that arises from the white and red luster of his body. It shines out to the horizon; it is so bright that even the gods cannot bear it.

The Kalki has excellent ministers, generals, and a great many queens. He has a bodyguard, elephants and elephant trainers, horses, chariots, and palanquins. His own wealth and the wealth of his subjects, the power of his magic spells, the nagas, demons, and goblins that serve him, the wealth offered to him by the centaurs, and the quality of his food are all such that even the lord of the gods cannot compete with him.

Since the Kalki has a great many queens, he has many sons and daughters. However, when the Kalki-to-be is born (it does not matter whether he is the oldest son or not) there is a rain of white lotus flowers, and for one week prior to his birth the crown prince's body emits light like a radiant jewel. The queen mother, a daughter of one of the ninety-six satraps of Shambhala, is distinguished by the fact that at the time of her birth a rain of blue lotuses falls and a huge, previously unknown flower grows in front of her home. The Kalki and his queens possess the four aims of life: sensual pleasure, wealth, ethics, and liberation. They never become sick or old, and although they always enjoy sensual pleasure, their virtue never decreases. The Kalki does not have more than one or two heirs, but he has many daughters who are given as vajra ladies during the initiations held on the full moon of *Caitra* each year.

Each of the eight lotus petals of Shambhala has 120 million villages in it. Thus, adding them all together there are 960 million villages in Shambhala. Each ten million villages is governed by a satrap, so there are ninety-six satraps. The satraps teach the Kalachakra as long as the Buddha's Dharma endures. Most of them are adept at magic spells. Each of the ninety-six satraps has a magical staff; when the staff is given to a messenger, the messenger instantaneously arrives wherever the satrap wishes.

The houses in the 960 million villages of Shambhala are pleasant two-story houses similar to the houses in India. The people born in Shambhala have fine bodies and appearances, and they are very wealthy. Even those having relatively little wealth have near to a hundred treasuries full of jewels. The men of Shambhala wear caps, and white or red cotton clothes. Women wear white or blue garments pleated and patterned with beautiful designs.

The people of Shambhala live in accordance with very mild laws; beating and imprisonment are unknown. There is absolutely no sickness, famine, and so forth. The people are naturally good, intelligent, and inclined towards virtue. Most of the people born in Shambhala obtain buddhahood during that very life by means of the Guhyasamaja, Samvara, Hevajra, Kalachakra, or one of the other *Anuttara* Yoga tantra systems. Most have obtained samadhis such as are taught in the Perfection of Wisdom sutras. Even the laypeople's servants who do not practice meditation are able to advance to a pure land by transferring their consciousnesses at the time of death. No one is born into an evil state of existence from Shambhala.

The clergy, and the various sacred receptacles of body, speech, and mind (such as images, texts, stupas, and so on) receive measureless honor and worship in Shambhala. It seems that most of the monks there are provided with naga or demon servants through the power of magic spells, but in general the clergy does not possess fine things. They go bare-headed and barefoot, and only keep the three vestments and the mendicant's bowl and staff; they are extremely faithful towards even the minor Vinaya vows.

All the authentic Buddhist doctrines that exist in the southern continent, *Jambudvipa*, (that includes the earth) are in Shambhala. From the minor practices of the eighteen Vaibhasika schools, such as the ordained person's rule about rinsing the mouth before and after meals, on through the scriptures and commentaries of the four classes of Mahayana tantras, all are there. In particular, the teachings of Tsong kha pa and his disciples have been magically carried to Shambhala from Tibet by heroes, wizards, and the Kalkis of Shambhala.

SUCHANDRA[5]

There is little recorded about the history of Shambhala prior to Suchandra. We are told the names of his father and mother, Suryaprabha and Vijaya, and that the dynasty of Shambhala belongs to the same Shakya line into which Shakyamuni Buddha was born, but that is about all. However, later events will show that the religion of Shambhala prior to Suchandra's introduction of the Kalachakra belonged to the Indian Vedic tradition.

King Suchandra, like King Indrabhuti of Uddiyana, was an emanation of the tenth-stage bodhisattva Vajrapani. This is significant because Vajrapani is the chief redactor of the Vajrayana teachings. Vajrapani and his various emanations serve as the intermediaries between the Buddha and ordinary human beings in the transmission of the Vajrayana doctrines.

After the Buddha taught the *Paramadibuddha* at Dhanyakataka, Suchandra and his satraps returned to Shambhala, as mentioned above. Suchandra then composed a sixty thousand line commentary on the *Paramadibuddha* using the language of Shambhala. Having erected the great Kalachakra mandala south of Kalapa, Suchandra offered initiation into, and explanation of, the Kalachakra system to the residents of the 960 million villages of Shambhala. Those who liked these teachings listened to them, recited them, memorized them, and in turn gave them to others. In the second year after he taught the tantra, Suchandra manifested various miraculous phenomena. Then, using an enjoyment body (sambho-gakaya), he returned to the place his emanation body (nirmana-kaya) had come from, as a cause for sentient beings' siddhis (attain-ments).

YASHAS AND PUNDARIKA[6]

The sources are silent about the careers of the next six kings of Shambhala. We are told only that they reigned for one hundred years each, teaching the Dharma and protecting their land. (See the Appendix for their names.)

However, the seventh Dharma King of Shambhala, Sureshana, and his queen Vishvamata give birth to a son who was to leave his mark on the subsequent history of Shambhala. He was called Yashas—"the Renowned."

King Yashas, an emanation of Manjushri, taught the Dharma on the bodhisattva's lion throne of Shambhala for one hundred years. Then, at the end of his reign, he knew that the time had come for the maturation of the 35 million brahman sages of Shambhala. By the power of his five psychic powers[7] he knew that the sages would obtain the noble path. On the full moon of *Phalguna* (February–March) King Yashas summoned the 35 million brahman sages, who were led by Suryaratha, to the mandala house south of Kalapa. There he gave them the following precept:

"O Suryaratha, and you other brahman sages, listen to my speech that bestows the excellence of omniscience! On this full moon of *Caitra* (next month) I must give the Vajrayana doctrine to you who observe the precepts of the Vedas and *smrtis*.[8] Thus, venerable sirs, separate out the brahmans belonging to the families of various other countries and show them to me."

Because of that statement, they scrutinized the practices of the various countries: eating from skulls, eating beef and buffalo flesh, drinking liquor, committing incest with one's mother, and so forth. When they saw that the countries' customs were mutually contradictory, they all fell down.

Thus, seeing their contradictions, King Yashas spoke:

"Here, I must enter you into this mandala house of Lord Kalachakra and give you the worldly and transcendental initiations. Furthermore, you venerable sirs must eat, drink, and form marriage relations with the vajra family, in accordance with my command. But if you will not obey my command, venerable sirs, then quit my 960 million villages and go wherever you will!

"Otherwise, after eight hundred years have elapsed, your sons, grandsons, and so forth will engage in the barbarian Dharma and will become teachers of the barbarian Dharma in the ninety-six great lands of Shambhala and so forth. Using the mantra of the barbarian deity Vishavimla[u] they will hack the throats of beasts with cleavers. Then they will enjoin eating the flesh of those beasts killed with the mantra of their own deity, and they will prohibit eating the flesh of beasts that die due to their own karma.

"Also, that Dharma is authoritative for you because of the statement in the *smrti*: 'Beasts are emitted for sacrifice.' There is no difference between the Vedic Dharma and the barbarian Dharma with regards to killing.

"Therefore, the sons, grandsons, and so forth of your family will see the valor of those barbarians, as well as the entrance of their devil deity into battle, and in the future, after eight hundred years have elapsed, they will become barbarians.

"Once they have joined the race of the barbarians, everyone dwelling in the 960 million villages, the four castes and so forth, will also become barbarians. For the brahman sages say: 'Where the great person goes, that is the path.'

"Here, in the barbarian Dharma as well as in the Vedic Dharma one must kill for the sake of the deity and the ancestors, and the same is true in the Dharma of the kshatriyas. For the brahmans say: 'Having satisfied the ancestors and the gods, there is no guilt in eating flesh,' and likewise: 'I see no fault in one who would do ill to a vicious beast.'

"Thus, holding the Vedic Dharma to be authoritative, they will take up the barbarian Dharma. For this reason, so that the barbarian Dharma will not enter Shambhala in the future, I give you this precept. Therefore, you venerable sirs must obey my command."

Spoken in such a fashion, King Yashas's speech, together with its chastising command, was like a lightning-bolt falling on the heads of the brahman sages. They said to Suryaratha: "O Suryaratha! Please inform the lord of the people, Yashas: 'We will not abandon the Dharma of race that is explained in the Vedas and engage in the Dharma of initiations of the vajra family. Therefore, in accordance with your command, it is best that we go to the land of the Aryans (India), south of the Sita River and the Himalayas, north of the island of Lamka (Sri Lanka)'."

Using the words of the brahman sages, Suryaratha informed the lord of the people Yashas: "O great king! Emperor! Supreme sovereign! You are fully endowed with the thirty-two major marks and the eighty minor marks of a great person! You are the ornament of the splendid Shakya family! Supremely compassionate one! Have mercy on those engaged in the Dharma of their own family! Since by all means we must obey your command, we will not engage in the initiations of the vajra family; it is best that, in accordance with your command, we go to the land of the Aryans south of the Sita River, between the Himalayas and the island of Lamka."

Then, because of Suryaratha's speech, King Yashas said: "Venerable sirs, quickly leave the land of Shambhala! In this way all the sentient beings dwelling in the 960 million villages north of the Sita River will completely abandon the non-virtuous karmic paths of killing and so forth. Then, by the blessing of Lord Kalachakra, they will obtain the path of right gnosis."

In accordance with King Yashas' command, all those brahman sages left the village of Kalapa. On the tenth day they entered into a forest.

Through the power of his five psychic powers, King Yashas knew that they had entered into the forest. He knew that should the brahman sages go to the land of the Aryans, all the sentient beings dwelling in the 960 million villages would have disastrous thoughts. The kshatriyas and other people would think: "Here, the reason the sages left is that the path spoken of in the Vajrayana is not the path of right gnosis. For this reason those sages have completely abandoned their own place, from fear of the splendid King Yashas. Taking their households, they have gone to the land of the Aryans. They all strive for liberation." Thinking this way the sentient beings would obtain ill fortune because their minds would become unsuitable vessels for the profound and extensive Dharma.

Thus, knowing the dispositions of the individual minds of all people, the lord of the people, Yashas became absorbed in the samadhi named "Stupefier of All the Families of Vishnu, Brahma, and Rudra." By means of that samadhi, and by the power of the deity's blessing, all the sages in the forest became stupefied. Aborigines and so forth dwelling in that forest bound all the sages, brought them back to the great mandala house, and threw them before the feet of the lord of the people, Yashas.

Awakening, they saw the lord of the people, Yashas, the mandala house, and the sandalwood pleasure grove. When they saw these things they were astonished, and said this: "Oh! This is very strange! Who brought us from the great forest back to the mandala house while we were unconscious?"

King Yashas' minister, Sagaramati, an emanation body, heard this speech of the brahman sages and said: "O Suryaratha and you other brahman sages, do not be astonished! This King Yashas is not parochial. He is a great, enraged bodhisattva who has appeared due to the blessing of the Buddha in order to take care of you. Therefore, go to his feet for refuge and request initiation into the path that achieves the worldly and transcendental siddhis in the King of Tantra—the Adibuddha!

Then, due to Sagaramati's speech and the blessing of the Buddha, Suryaratha and the other brahman sages were awakened, and said this: "Well said! Well said, Sagaramati! Your speech has awakened our minds. Therefore, now we will go for refuge to the Three Jewels and request initiation into the path that achieves the worldly and transcendental siddhis, in the King of Tantra—Kalachakra, so that all sentient beings may obtain true, complete buddhahood in this very life."

Having said that, the sages called to Suryaratha, king of the brahman family: "O Suryaratha! You are a single book that contains the texts of the Vedas and so forth! Your heart grasps that which is to be demonstrated in all the worldly and transcendental treatises! Thus, request King Yashas with our words of request! We too will go for refuge, preceeding it with a mandala, and then all of us will request instruction."

Then, in accordance with the speech of the brahman sages, Suryaratha made a mandala of flowers formed from jewels and gold. He scattered handfuls of jeweled flowers before the feet of the lord of the people, Yashas. Placing their knees on the ground and their hands on top of their heads, Suryaratha and the brahman sages bowed to the feet of Yashas. Then Suryaratha planted his right kneecap on the earth, set his cupped hands at his forehead, and requested the lord of the people, Yashas for instruction: "Please teach the King of Tantra—the Adibuddha! In it the Bhagavan explained that even those who created the five sins of immediate retribution[10] may obtain buddhahood in this very life. He explained that they will obtain the *mahamudra* that is governed by the supreme unchanging bliss of Bhagavan Vajradhara. Please redact this twelve thousand verse *Adibuddha* that the Tathagata taught to King Suchandra by making the text shorter, and compose a short *Adibuddha, King of Tantra*. Then, please teach it to the brahman sages."

King Yashas was pleased by the request of Suryaratha and the sages. On the full moon of *Caitra* he initiated the sages in the great Kalachakra mandala south of Kalapa. As the sages requested, Yashas taught them an abridgement of the *Paramadibuddha*. On the full moon of the following month, *Vaisakha* (April–May), the sages attained the supreme siddhi of *mahamudra*.

The abridged tantra (*laghutantra*) that Yashas taught the sages is called the *Sri Kalacakra*, and it is our basic tantra for the Kalachakra system.[11] Yashas later taught the sages an addendum to the *Sri Kalacakra* entitled *Sri Kalacakratantrottara Tantrahrdayanama* (Peking #5). The *Tantrahrdayam* contains, among other things, some fascinating and obscure prophecies. Yashas also taught the sages an extremely abbreviated form of the *Sri Kalacakra* from the point of view of vajrayoga. This text, the *Kalacakralaghutantrarajahrdaya Nama*, is only extant in the Lhasa edition of the Tibetan *Kanjur* (#373). Another text redacted by Yashas is the *Sri Kalacakranama Tantragarbha* (Peking #6). This text is a condensation of the *Paramadibuddha*'s *sadangayoga* sadhana.

All four of the preceding texts are mainly composed of the

speech of the Buddha, (*buddhavacanam*). Yashas was primarily the redactor of these texts; only in a derivative sense was he the teacher of them.

However, two treatises independently authored by Yashas have come down to us: the *Pradarsanumatoddesapariksa nama* (Peking #4610), and the *Triyogahrdayaprakasa nama* (Peking #2087). With the all-important exception of the *Sri Kalacakra*, none of the texts listed above are known to have survived in the original Sanskrit.

Yashas's conversion of the brahman sages was to have an important impact on the subsequent history of Shambhala. By combining all the castes of Shambhala into one vajra family, Yashas became Kalki, the lineage king of Shambhala. The Buddha had prophesied this in the *Paramadibuddha*:

> *vagmi vajrakule yena tena vajrakuli yasah/*
> *caturvarnaikakalkena kalki brahmakulena na//*

"Vagmi Yashas, possessing the vajra family, will become Kalki by making the four castes into a single clan, (*kalkah*), within the vajra family, not by making them into a brahman family."

By becoming Kalki, Yashas ensured that Shambhala will remain outside the range of the barbarian depredations. In particular, he ensured that his descendant Kalki, Raudra Chakri, and the armies of Shambhala will perform their role at the end of the current Age of Strife, the *Kaliyuga*.

Yashas and his queen Tara had a son named Pundarika, who was an emanation of Avalokiteshvara. In accordance with a prophecy made by the Buddha in the *Paramadibuddha*, Yashas appointed Pundarika as the second Kalki and ordered him to write a commentary on the *Sri Kalacakra*; then Yashas passed away. Kalki Pundarika followed his father's command and wrote the *Vimalaprabha*.

This huge commentary (together with the *Sri Kalacakra*) is our basic textual source for the Kalachakra system as a whole. We are very fortunate that the *Vimalaprabha*, like the *Sri Kalacakra*, survives in the original Sanskrit.

Two other works by Kalki Pundarika have also come down to us. The *Kalacakratantragarbha vrtti vimalaprabha nama* (Peking #4608) is a short but important commentary on the *Tantragarbha* (Peking #6), mentioned above. Pundarika's *Sri Paramarthaseva* (Peking #2065) is an independent composition, entirely in verse, that is mainly concerned with ethics and yoga. Fragments of the *Paramarthaseva* exist in Sanskrit.

The rule of the Kalkis subsequent to Pundarika seems to have been fairly uneventful. At any rate the literature has little to say about their activities.

INDIA

With the introduction of the Kalachakra into India we come into first contact with "history" as defined by western-style historical science. There are indications that some form of an Adibuddha/Kalachakra tantra was known in India prior to the period we will discuss,[12] but for practical purposes we can safely say that the Kalachakra system first openly appeared in India at the beginning of the 11th century A.D.

This period is established by two facts: 1. The main basic texts of the Kalachakra system used by the Indians, the *Sri Kalacakra* and the *Vimalaprabha*, contain a date that can be calculated as 1012 A.D.[13] This date forms the basis for all the astronomical calculations in the Kalachakra *laghukaranam*. Although this date does not necessarily represent the exact year of the composition of these texts, the mathematics of the Kalachakra astronomy and a great deal of other internal evidence certify that these texts were composed around this time. 2. The vajracharyas responsible for the early propagation of the Kalachakra in India can all be dated to the beginning of the 11th century, insofar as they can be dated at all. This will be demonstrated below.

Unlike most Vajrayana systems, we are able to establish a fairly narrow temporal frame of reference for the introduction and early spread of the Kalachakra. However, the exact circumstances of these events are far from clear. The Tibetan historians, our main sources, repeat a mass of Indian stories that cannot be easily reconciled with one another. As one Tibetan historian rather diplomatically put it, "In general, it is possible that even the stories of the Indians are uncertain."[14] A comparison of all the different Tibetan histories would show that some Tibetans also added to the confusion.

Part of the apparent confusion in the Indian stories can be traced to the fact that some Indian vajracharyas went by more than one name, whereas in other cases two or more gurus were called by the same name. As a general principle this is accepted by both the Tibetan and the western-style historians.

Another cause of variation in the Indian accounts is the manner of transmission. As we will see later, the Kalachakra went from India to Tibet via a number of different guru lineages. Thus, the Tibetans studied under Indian masters who were themselves various stages removed from the original Indian source of the Kalachakra. Given this, and the fact that these were oral traditions until the Tibetans wrote them down much later, it is not surprising that we are presented with a number of different versions of the Indian origins of the Kalachakra.

In what follows I will give a translation of one important source for the history of the Kalachakra in India.[15] Bu ston Rin chen grub set this account in writing in 1329, making it the oldest dated source to my knowledge. Even so, Bu ston did not invent these stories. Rather, he drew them, probably verbatim, from earlier sources that are not available to us. Bu ston's account describes the Indian origins of two traditions: the "Rwa tradition"—the Kalachakra tradition introduced into Tibet by the Nepalese pandit Samantashribhadra and the Tibetan translator Rwa Chos rab; and the "'Bro tradition"—the tradition introduced by the Kashmiri pandit Somanatha and the translator 'Bro Shes rab grags. ("Rwa" and "'Bro" are names of Tibetan clans.) Following the translation I will present and discuss some information drawn from other sources that I hope will shed light on certain obscure points in the translation.

According to the Rwa tradition, the Kalachakra and related commentaries famed as the *Bodhisattva Corpus* appeared in India during the simultaneous reigns of three kings. Taking the area known as Vajrasana (Bodh Gaya in present-day Bihar) as the center, the three kings were: Dehapala, the Master of Elephants, in the East; Jaugangapa, the Master of Humans, in the South; and Kanauj, the Master of Horses, in the West. At that time the great pandit Cilu (Tsi lu), who mastered all aspects of the Buddha's Dharma, was born in Orissa, one of the five countries of eastern India. Cilu studied all the Buddhist texts at the Ratnagiri *vihara* (northeast of modern-day Cuttack in Orissa), at Vikramasila, and at Nalanda (Na Lendra).

In particular, he studied at the Ratnagiri *vihara* that was undamaged by the Turks. Cilu realized that, in general, in order to achieve buddhahood in a single life he would need the Mantrayana, and in particular, that he would need the clarifications of these doctrines contained in the *Bodhisattva Commentaries*. Knowing that these teachings were extant in Shambhala, and depending on the instruction of his deity, he joined up with traders who sought jewels in the ocean. Having agreed with the traders, who were setting out across the sea, to meet up after six months, they went separate ways.

Cilu proceeded in stages and finally, upon climbing a mountain, he met a man. The man asked him, "Where are you going?" Cilu replied, "I am going to Shambhala in search of the *Bodhisattva Corpus*." The man said, "It is extremely difficult to go there, but if you can understand it, you could listen to it even here." Cilu realized that the man was an emanation of Manjushri. Cilu prostrated, offered a mandala, and requested instruction. The man conferred all the initiations, the tantra commentaries, and the oral instructions on Cilu. He grasped Cilu, placed a flower on top of his head, and blessed him, saying, "Realize the entire *Bodhisattva Corpus!*"

Thus, like water poured from one vessel into another, Cilu realized the entire *Bodhisattva Corpus*. He went back the way he had come and, meeting with the traders, he returned to eastern India.

Another tradition, possibly Rwa, has it that the pandit Cilu was the son of a yogi and that his father led him to Shambhala. There they met a monk having a handsome appearance, an emanation of Avalokiteshvara. By his blessing Cilu was able to memorize a thousand verses each day. Having memorized all the tantra commentaries, he returned to India where he became renowned by his ordination name, "Cilupa" (Tsi lu pa).

Later Cilupa resided in the capital of the king of Kataka (Ka ta ka; present-day Cuttack in Orissa). He had three disciples. Because the disciples asked him to write the tantra commentaries down in a volume, he did so. One of the disciples remained ordinary, but another, *Jinakaragupta (rGyal ba'i 'byung gnas sbas pa) gained siddhi. The third, "Pido acharya" (or below, Pinda acharya), born in Bengal in eastern India, became a great scholar who comprehended and experienced the entire *Bodhisattva Corpus*.

At that time another king made war on Kataka, so the master
and his disciples hid all the texts of the tantra commentaries in a
pit and fled. When the war subsided and they looked for the books,
they found that the last halves of the commentaries on the Samvara
and the Hevajra tantras were missing. The disciples asked Cilupa to
rewrite the missing portions, but he refused, saying that since the
dakinis had hidden them it was improper to write them again.
Cilupa then returned to eastern India.

Later, Pinda acarya taught the *Bodhisattva Corpus* to acharya
*Kalachakrapada the Elder (Dus zhabs pa chen po) who was born
in Varendra (northern Bengal). *Kalachakrapada the Elder understood and experienced the teachings as the previous masters had.

Some say that *Kalachakrapada was able to ask for whatever he
wished due to a vision of Tara, and that in dependence on the
instructions of Tara he went to Shambhala. On the way he was met
by Avalokiteshvara, who led him to the mandala house in the
sandalwood grove of Kalapa. There he was initiated and given
explanations of the tantra commentaries, together with the books
that contained them. *Kalachakrapada returned to eastern India
and lived at *Phullahari (Me tog khyim). Among his disciples the
four best were *Kalachakrapada the Younger (Dus zhabs chung ba),
*Vinayakaramati ('Dul ba 'byung gnas blos gros), *Simhadvaja
(Seng ge rgyal mtshan), and *Ananta (mTha' yas).

*Kalachakrapada the Younger was born in the east in the Man-
juha region (Northern Bengal?). He was also called "Bodhipa," and
"Nalendrapa" as well. Some hold that he was identical with Dharmakara, but this is unacceptable because Dharmakara was the disciple of Sadhuputra, and therefore is later. The Rwa tradition says
that *Kalachakrapada the Younger taught the *Bodhisattva Corpus* to
Ratnakara, who propagated it at Nalanda. However, previous lamas
have said that the two were friends, and that *Kalachakrapada the
Younger erected a Kalachakra temple at Nalanda and attracted
many pandits as his disciples. These lamas said that since this
correlates with other lineages, there is no need to mention Ratnakara.

*Kalachakrapada the Younger thought that if the Kalachakra
was propagated in Magadha it would spread everywhere. During
the period when The One Having A Wooden Seat (? Shing stan
can) was ruling Magadha and the Sendhapas[16] controlled Otanta-

puri *vihara*, *Kalachakrapada the Younger went to Nalanda. Above the door of the *vihara* he drew the mantra of The One Possessing Power In Ten Aspects (*dasakaravasi; rnam bcu dbang ldan*). Below the mantra he wrote:

> Those who do not know the *Paramadibuddha*, do not know the *Namasamgiti*. Those who do not know the *Namasamgiti*, do not know the Gnosis Body of Vajradhara. Those who do not know the Gnosis Body of Vajradhara, do not know the Mantrayana. All those who do not know the Mantrayana, are samsaric: they are separate from the path of Bhagavan Vajradhara.[17]

About five hundred pandits living at Nalanda were displeased with this, and debated with *Kalachakrapada the Younger. But he defeated them all with the profound and vast nature of the Kalachakra doctrines, and they became his disciples. In particular, Manjukirti, Abhiyukta, Pandit *Parvata (Ri bo pa), *Da Bodhisattva (Da byang chub sems dpa'), Abhaya, *Mahapunya (Punya chen po), Gambhira the Kashmiri, Santagupta, Gunaraksita, Somanatha, rTsa mi (Sangs rgyas grags pa, a.k.a. Buddhakirti, of Mi nyag), and other scholars became his disciples. Even the royal family, the kshatriyas, and the merchants had such faith that they copied texts and created the causes of their future realization of the doctrines. In this way the Kalachakra became widely spread. Later Pandit Samantashribhadra, born in Patan (Ye rang) in Nepal, heard the Kalachakra taught by five masters, and in particular followed Manjukirti.

According to the 'Bro tradition, the Kalachakra was brought to India during the reign of Kalki Shripala. A couple who practised the yoga of Yamantaka, duly performed the ritual for the birth of a son as it is given in the *Yamantaka Tantra*, and had a son. When he grew up he learned that in the North the bodhisattvas themselves taught the Dharma, and he went to listen to them. With his psychic power Kalki Shripala knew of the youth's pure motivation and enthusiasm for the profound Dharma. The Kalki knew that if the youth attempted to come to Shambhala it would endanger his life because of the waterless wasteland that takes four months to cross. Shripala used an emanation body to meet the youth at the edge of the desert.

The Kalki asked the youth, "Where are you going, and why?"

When the youth told him his intention, the Kalki said, "That road is very difficult. But if you can understand these things, couldn't you listen to them even here?" The youth realized that this was an emanation of the Kalki, and asked him for instruction. Right there the Kalki initiated the youth, and for four months he taught him all the *Anuttara* tantras, especially the three inner *Bodhisattva Corpus* commentaries. Like a vase filled to the brim, the youth realized and memorized all the tantras. When he returned to India he became renowned as an emanation of Manjushri, and his name was "*Kalachakrapada."

At that time in India there was a very dull monk who wanted to increase his intelligence. Depending upon the instructions he received from his deity in a dream, he made an image of the goddess Kurukulla out of coral and inserted it in the mouth of a woman's corpse. Sitting cross-legged on her back, he practised sadhana for seven days. The corpse's face looked up, and she said, "What do you want?" Although he wanted to be able to memorize all that he read, due to his stupidity he said that he wanted to be able to memorize all that he wrote. The corpse said, "So be it." From this he was called Pandit Vagishvarakirti (Ngag gi dbang phyugs grags pa; "The Renowned Lord of Speech"). He lived at the *vihara* of Khasarpana, and once he asked the acharya *Kalachakrapada, "How many tantras do you know?" The acharya answered, "I know this and that," but it is said that the pandit could not remember even the names of the tantras!

*Kalachakrapada had many disciples, and most of them became yogis. From among them, the one who maintained the tradition of teaching was his disciple Nalendrapa, who was also renowned as "*Kalachakrapada the Younger." He is said to have possessed qualities equaling his guru's. Some accounts say *Kalachakrapada the Younger and Nalendrapa were guru and disciple.

At that time Somanatha, the very intelligent son of a brahman, was born in Kashmir. For twelve years he learned his father's heretic Dharmas, but his mother was a Buddhist and she told him that he should study her religion. She put him under the tutelage of the Kashmiri pandit called "*Brahmanapada" (Bram ze zhabs). Since Somanatha was very handsome, the pandit's daughter said, "You must have intercourse with me in order to listen to the Dharma." Somanatha accepted that and listened to a lot of Buddhist Dharma.

At that time *Kalachakrapada the Elder's disciple, *Vinayakara-mati (Dul ba'i blo gros), sent the *Sekoddesa* and a commentary on the *Sekaprakriya* to *Brahmanapada.[18] *Brahmanapada showed them to Somanatha, who read them and admired them a lot. Somanatha went to Magadha, met the Elder and Younger *Kalachakrapadas, and received instruction on all of the three *Bodhisattva Corpus* commentaries.

At that time Somanatha became involved in a debate with the Kashmiri scholar *Ratnavajra (Rin chen rdo rje), and Somanatha won. *Ratnavajra told Somanatha that he should go elsewhere lest *Ratnavajra's disciples lose faith. Somanatha, thinking that he would spread the Kalachakra in Tibet, acquiesced, and this is what he did.

* * * * *

The Rwa and 'Bro traditions give divergent accounts of the Indian origins of the Kalachakra. The Rwa tradition in particular seems to be divided into a number of opinions about the introduction of the Kalachakra into India. Nevertheless, we can simplify and schematize the Rwa and 'Bro lineages as follows:

Rwa	'Bro
An Emanation of Manjushri or Avalokiteshvara	
↓	
Cilu (Cilupa)	
↓	
Pindo (Pinda, Pindi, Pido)	Kalki Shripala
↓	↓
*Kalachakrapada the Elder	— *Kalachakrapada the Elder
↓	↓
*Kalachakrapada the Younger (a.k.a. Bodhipa and Nalendrapa)	Nalendrapa (a.k.a. *Kalachakrapada the Younger)
↓	↓
Manjukirti	→ Somanatha
↓	↓
Samantashribhadra	'Bro Shes rab grags
↓	
Rwa Chos Rab	

Taking the Rwa lineage first, it is worth noting that none of the
Kalkis in the time frame we are considering (after Pundarika and
before Raudra Chakri—see Appendix) are emanations of either
Manjushri or Avalokiteshvara. Likewise, Cilu is a particularly obscure individual. There are two works clearly attributed to him in
the Tibetan *Tanjur*: a commentary on the *Guhyasamaja* (Peking
#2709), and a short instruction on the *sadangayoga* (Peking #2090).
But neither of these texts is intrinsically related to the Kalachakra
or the *Bodhisattva Corpus*.

When we reach Pindo, however, things are quite different.[19] The
Bengali guru Dipamkarashrijnana, better known as Atisha (ca.
982–1054), refers to "the great Adibuddha tantra" in his famous
Bodhipathapradipa.[20] In his auto-commentary to the *Bodhipathapradipa*, Atisha informs us that this reference to the *Paramadibuddha* derives from the oral instructions of his guru Pindo (bSod
snyoms pa).[21] Atisha also tells us that his guru Pindo was a monk,
and that he came from Suvarnadvipa (gSer gling), i.e., Java (Yava-
dvipa; Ya ba di pa). This information correlates nicely with the
colophon to the *Sri Kalacakragarbhalankara nama Sadhana* (Peking
#2081). This sadhana, one of the oldest Kalachakra translations in
the Tibetan *Tanjur*, was written by "the great scholar, the brahman
Pindo (bSod snyoms pa), who was born in the land of the southern
ocean."

I think Pindo's having been born in Java, "the land of the
southern ocean," explains an otherwise very strange statement
appearing in a prayer of the 'Bro Kalachakra tradition. This prayer,
recorded by Bu ston, requests the blessings of "Kalki Shripala at the
end of the southern ocean."[22] Thus, I think Kalki Shripala is
another name for Pindo.

I also think that the identification of Kalki Shripala with Pindo
would harmonize with Taranatha's assertion in his *History of Buddhism in India* that, "Pindo (Pi to) acharya introduced the Kalachakra tantra during the second half of Mahipala's lifetime."[23] The
Mahipala referred to by Taranatha must be the Pata king Mahipala I (reigned ca. 988–1038). I do not think it is mere coincidence
that Kalki Dripala was the successor of Kalki Mahipala in the
dynasty of Shambhala (see Appendix). If, as I too believe, Pindo
introduced the Kalachakra into India during the reign of Mahipala, it would have been a stroke of genius to make the reigning

Kalki of Shambhala have the same name as the reigning monarch in eastern India.

The Rwa and 'Bro accounts translated above make it clear that the Kalachakra system first appeared in India in conjunction with the *Bodhisattva Corpus* (Byang chub sems dpa'i skor). These three tantra commentaries are:

1) *Vimalaprabha* by Kalki Pundarika
2) *Hevajrapindarthatika* (Peking #2310) by Bodhisattva Vajra-garbha
3) *Laksabhidhanaduddhrtalaghutantrapindarthavivarana   nama* (Peking #2117) by Bodhisattva Vajrapani

These texts comment on the abridged tantras (*laghutantra*) of the Kalachakra, Hevajra, and Samvara systems respectively. Also, the latter two commentaries explain their tantras in accordance with the special ideas of the Kalachakra. All three commentaries have stylistic and doctrinal features in common, including passages that correspond verbatim. All three refer to and cite the *Paramadi-buddha*. The latter two commentaries are called *pindarthatika* and *pindarthavivarana*. As the Tibetan translators have shown, these phrases both mean, "a commentary on the condensed meaning." But perhaps they can also be translated as, "a commentary according to the thought of Pindo."

If we accept the identification of Kalki Shripala with Pindo, the Rwa and 'Bro traditions would agree that he was the teacher of *Kalachakrapada the Elder. In fact I would go one step further, and put forward the proposition that *Kalachakrapada is yet another name for Pindo. I base this idea on a very valuable piece of histori-cal data, the translator's colophon to Pundarika's *Kalacakratantra (garbha) vrtti vimalaprabha nama* (Peking #4608). This colophon was written by Gyi jo Zla ba'i 'od zer, who translated the text under the guidance of the Indian pandit Shri Bhadrabodhi. I translate this colophon as follows:

> The one called "*Kalachakra" (Dus kyi 'khor lo pa) went to the land of Shambhala (Sam ba la) and gained mas-tery of the psychic powers. The one called "Nado" (Na ro pa), a brahman by caste, born in the land of Uddi-yana (U rgyan), was the successor in his (i.e., *Kala-chakra's) lineage; he was born from shakti and author-

ized by the deity. The guru (Shri Bhadrabodhi) was of
his (i.e.,*Nado's) caste; he heard the tantra, he was
taught by the heavenly deity. By listening to him and
making effort to translate this commentary, may I
obtain the state of fearless bliss.

Gyi jo Zla ba'i 'od zer was probably the first Tibetan to translate
texts on Kalachakra. He was active in the middle of the 11th century,
as is evident from the translation work he performed under Atisha.
We can schematize Gyi jo's Kalachakra lineage as follows:

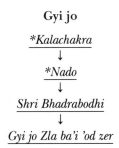

Gyi jo

*Kalachakra
↓
*Nado
↓
Shri Bhadrabodhi
↓
Gyi jo Zla ba'i 'od zer

*Nado, better known by the Tibetan spelling of his name—
Naropa, passed away *circa* 1030 A.D.[24] We know that *Nado was a
master of the Kalachakra; this is evident from the large commentary he wrote on the *Sekoddesa.* If this is the case, then why doesn't he
appear in the Kalachakra lineages put forward by the Rwa and 'Bro
traditions?

In fact he does appear. As Bu ston tells us, Gyi jo Zla ba'i 'od
zer's guru, Shri Bhadrabodhi was the disciple of *Kalachakrapada
(Dus zhabs).[25] Thus, *Nado was called *Kalachakrapada the
Younger, and Nalendrapa (the man of Nalanda), within the early
Kalachakra cult in India. The former name is applicable because,
as Gyi jo tells us, *Nado was the lineage holder of *Kalachakra, who
brought the Kalachakra to India from Shambhala. The latter name
certainly fits *Nado, the crest jewel of the contemporary Nalanda
vajracaryas.

To summarize all of the preceeding discussion, I put forward
my own notion of one aspect of the early transmission of the Kalachakra in India:

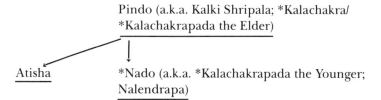

Pindo (a.k.a. Kalki Shripala; *Kalachakra/ *Kalachakrapada the Elder)

Atisha

*Nado (a.k.a. *Kalachakrapada the Younger; Nalendrapa)

There are no obstacles to this theory from the point of view of chronology because Atisha was a younger contemporary and associate of both Pindo and Nado. Also, I accept Taranatha's assertion that Pindo introduced the Kalachakra during the last half of Mahipala's lifetime, and it makes sense that the great *Nado would have studied this extraordinary doctrine directly under the guru who introduced it.

Even if the above theory turns out to be correct, it only accounts for one aspect of the early spread of the Kalachakra in India. The Kalachakra literature in the *Tanjur* is evidence of the dynamics of a school. It could not be the product of merely one or two individuals.

To give just one example to illustrate this point: Anupamarakshita is revered by many Tibetan lamas as the most eminent Indian fountainhead of the Kalachakra *sadangayoga* precepts. Yet he does not appear (under this name, at least) in the Kalachakra lineages examined above. Anupamarakshita must have been among the earliest masters of the Kalachakra because *Nado cites him as an authority. Also, Anupamarakshita's *Sadangayoga* (Peking #2102) contains a block of twenty-four verses that also appear in the first "Brief Account" (*uddesa*) of the *Vimalaprabha*. Obviously, much more research is needed before we can say much that is definite about the history of the Kalachakra in India.

The history of the Kalachakra in India cannot be separated from the history of later Indian Vajrayana Buddhism as a whole. And, from the point of view of western-style historical science, a history of Indian Vajrayana Buddhism remains to be written. But one thing is clear: from the introduction of the *Bodhisattva Corpus* early in the 11th century until Buddhism as an organized religion was wiped out by Central Asian barbarians during the 13th and 14th centuries, the Kalachakra captured the imaginations of Vajrayana Buddhists in north India. Renowned vajracaryas composed an

extensive literature dealing with it, and, in certain sense, the Kalachakra can be seen as the culmination of Indian Vajrayana
Buddhism.

It was during this period also that the Kalachakra became an
international religious phenomenon. From the great monastic universities of Magadha, Bengal, and Orissa, it went east and south to
Burma and the Indonesian archipelago. Similarly, the Kalachakra
was carried north to Kashmir, Nepal, and Tibet, and from Tibet it
eventually spread to Mongolia and China.

TIBET[26]

The Kalachakra was transmitted from India into Tibet via a
number of different guru lineages from the 11th through the 14th
century. As mentioned previously, two of the most important lineages are styled the "Rwa tradition" and the "'Bro tradition."

According to Bu ston, the translator Rwa Chos rab traveled to
central Nepal (probably Patan) where he studied under the pandit
Samantashri for five years, ten months, and five days. Having mastered all the Kalachakra doctrines, Chos rab invited his guru to
Tibet where together they continued the work of translating the
various texts and disseminating the teachings. The Rwa tradition
continued in Tibet through Rwa Chos rab's son and grandson.

The 'Bro tradition originated from the visit of the Kashmiri
pandit Somanatha to Tibet. Together with 'Bro Shes rab grags,
Somanatha translated the *Vimalaprabha* into Tibetan and established this important teaching and practice lineage. By the middle
of the 14th century the *Sri Kalacakra* had been translated into
Tibetan fifteen or sixteen times; the *Vimalaprabha* more than ten.
This is really remarkable given the size and complexity of these
texts. No other Buddhist text received a comparable amount of
attention from the great Tibetan translators.

The Rwa and 'Bro lineages continued through successions of
teachers and eventually flowed together. One particularly notewor-
thy name from this period is that of Bu ston Rin chen grub (1290–
1364). Bu ston is perhaps best known for his part in the editing of
the Tibetan canon, but later lamas especially praised him for his
key role in the preservation of all of the different types of tantra

exposition and practice.[27] Bu ston made a close study of the Kalachakra; he produced a revised, annotated edition of the canonical
translations of the *Sri Kalacakra* and the *Vimalaprabha*. He also
wrote a number of important monographs on special topics in the
Kalachakra.

rJe Tsong kha pa bLo bzang grags pa (1357-1419), founder of
the dGe lug pa school, studied the Kalachakra under a disciple of
Bu ston. Tsong kha pa in turn transmitted it to his disciple mKhas
grub dGe legs dpal bzang (1385-1438). mKhas grub mastered the
entire Kalachakra system and composed a commentary on the
Vimalaprabha that is enormous even by Tibetan literary standards.
Entitled *The Illuminator of Reality* (*De kho na nyid snang bar byed pa*), it
occupies three large volumes in his collected works.

The dGe lug pa school maintained the study and practice of the
Kalachakra over the centuries. The Panchen Lamas of the
Tashilhunpo monastery in gTsang were especially active in the
practice of the Kalachakra. At Tashilhunpo there was a special
school devoted to the Kalachakra (*Dus 'khor grwa tshang*).

The third Panchen Lama, bLo bzang dpal ldan ye shes (1738-
1780), composed a prayer in which he expressed the wish to be
born in Shambhala during the reign of Kalki Raudra Chakri.[28] He
also wrote a book that came to be known as the *Guidebook to Shambhala* (*Sambha la'i lam yig*).[29] In addition to a more general account of
Asian history and geography, the book describes the route to Shambhala and the means by which a person can travel there. This
portion of the book is based, to a great extent, on another "guidebook" translated from Sanskrit, the *Kalapavatara*, (*Entrance to
Kalapa*), the capital of Shambhala; Peking #5908).

rGyal ba 'Jam dpal rgya mtsho, the 8th Dalai Lama (1758-1805),
introduced the Kalachakra into his personal monastery, the rNam
rgyal grwa tshang. From that time to the present, the rNam rgyal
grwa tshang has continued the study and practice of the Kalachakra, including the full complement of the intricate Kalachakra
rituals. His Holiness Tenzin Gyatso, the 14th Dalai Lama, belongs to
a Kalachakra lineage that traces itself back to the teaching of the
Paramadibuddha at Shri Dhanyakataka. His Holiness has been extremely generous in making this religious tradition available to the
people of the West.

At present the Kalachakra tradition appears to be in danger of

extinction. Due to the extreme complexity of this tantra, its masters
have never been numerous. Today, following the Chinese of inva-
sion of Tibet, their number has dwindled to a handful of refugees
in India.

THE FUTURE[30]

The eventual disintegration and disappearance of Buddhism is
not unexpected within the Buddhist view of history. A number of
sutras prophesy the decline of the Dharma and human life in
general during the end of the current age, and predict the glorious
coming of Maitreya Buddha in the distant future.

The Kalachakra tradition has a different vision of the future of
the world. It too depicts a steady degeneration of the world in
conjunction with the disappearance of virtuous forms of religion.
In the Kalachakra this period of decadance is synchronous with a
steady increase of the powers of evil in the form of barbarians
allied with demons. However, unlike the Maitreya prophecies, the
Kalachakra does not predict the total extinction of Buddhism, for
it teaches that the Buddhadharma will be preserved in Shambhala
out of the reach of the barbarians. When conditions finally reach
their nadir at the very end of the current Kali age, a great war will
erupt in which the army of Shambhala will do battle with the evil
barbarians and demons.

Conditions south of the Shita River will continue to degenerate
until the last Kalki, Raudra Chakri, ascends the lion throne of
Shambhala. Raudra Chakri, "The Wrathful One with the Wheel,"
will teach the Buddhadharma for almost fifty years, but then the
impending conflict between good and evil will come to a head. By
that time the southern half of Jambudvipa, that which is south of
the Shita River, will have come under the control of the barbarian
overlord Krinmati. Centered in Dili (Delhi) in western India,
Krinmati and his vassals will set their sights on the conquest of
Shambhala.

When Raudra Chakri sees the wild barbarians preparing to
attack, he will enter into an unwavering trance called "The
Samadhi of the Supreme Horse." While Raudra is absorbed in this
trance, his vast army will gather. Raudra and his generals, Hanu-

man and Rudra, will command an army of truly gigantic proportions. It will have 90 million cavalry mounted on horses swift as the
wind, four hundred thousand battle-intoxicated elephants, five
hundred thousand golden chariots, and uncountable infantry, all
brightly caparisoned. Composed of six divisions, the army will be
led by the ninety-six satraps of Shambhala. However, this war will
involve more than mere earthly forces, for the demons will side
with the barbarians, and Raudra Chakri will be assisted by the
twelve great gods: Hari (Vishnu), Nairrti, Vayu, Yama, Agni, Shan-
mukha (Skandha), Kubera, Shakra (Indra), Brahma, Rudra (Shiva),
Samudra, and Ganesha.

The army of Shambhala will come out of Kalapa and travel
south of the Shita River to India—there the great war will erupt.
Kalki Raudra Chakri will strike down the barbarian overlord
Krinmati, and Hanuman and Rudra will overcome the barbarian
commanders. Raudra Chakri's skilled and heroic archers will
defeat the barbarian infantry, the ninety-six satraps of Shambhala
will conquer the barbarian captains, the horses of Shambhala will
rout the barbarian cavalry, and the elephants of Shambhala will
crush the barbarian elephants. In particular, the twelve great gods
will destroy the demonic deities of the barbarians, and the forces of
evil will be completely eradicated. Having utterly destroyed the
barbarians, Raudra Chakri and his divine entourage will return to
Kalapa, the city on Mount Kailasha created by the gods.

Raudra Chakri's achievement of complete dominion will mark
the beginning of an Age of Perfection (*Kritayuga*). Human lifespan
will increase, and people will abandon evil behavior and only
cultivate virtue. They will enjoy good ethics, sensual pleasure,
wealth, and spiritual liberation. Grain will grow in the wild without
cultivation, and trees will perpetually bear fruit. A special feature
of this period is that during it a practitioner can achieve the highest siddhi through the Kalachakra with relative ease. Consequently,
the earth will become populated with Vajrayana adepts; even those
with lesser abilities will make great progress on the Mahayana path.

The great *chakravartin* Raudra Chakri will live to be a hundred
years old. At the end of his reign he will appoint his elder son
Brahma as the lord of Shambhala and his younger son Suresha as
master of the lands south of the Shita River. Having done this,

Raudra Chakri—last of the Kalkis, will return to the abode of bliss from which he came.

During the reigns of Brahma and his son Kashyapa, the average human lifespan will be nine hundred years. It will diminish during the subsequent reigns, and at the same time divisions based on caste will reappear. As a result of this disintegration, in accordance with the cycles of time, the various types of humans—royalty, sages, and barbarians—will appear again, and, again, the *chakravartin* will appear to subdue and reunify them.

Having read the preceding brief account of the eschatological doctrines contained in the Kalachakra, it is worthwhile to remember that, like everything else in this intricate system, they operate on more than one level of meaning. The "Great War" and the Age of Perfection that follows it can be interpreted literally as external historical events predicted to occur in about four hundred years.

However, the *Sri Kalacakra* and the *Vimalaprabha* give another, allegorical interpretation of the same myth. Here we find the elements of the Kalachakra apocalypse identified with the forces of gnosis and nescience within the Kalachakra practitioner. When a yogi conquers ignorance by means of the method and wisdom actualized in the Kalachakra vajrayoga, then the inner devils, demons, and barbarians that make samsaric life miserable are destroyed, and the Age of Perfection of complete enlightenment is produced. This is wholly in keeping with the fundamental structure of the Kalachakra system: the Outer Wheel of Time, i. e., the cosmos, is a reflection of the Inner Wheel of Time, i. e., a person's soul or psychophysical constituents. These worlds form the basis that is purified by the Other Wheel of Time, the soteriological path of apotheosis produced by the generation and completion processes of the Kalachakra vajrayoga.

APPENDIX: THE DYNASTY OF SHAMBHALA[31]

King	Emanation of Bodhisattva/ Wrathful King (wk)
Suryaprabha (and Queen Vijaya)	Vighnashakta (wk)

Dharma King

1)	Suchandra	Vajrapani
2)	Sureshvara (a.k.a. Suresha)	Kshitigarbha
3)	Teji	Yamantaka (wk)
4)	Somadatta	Sarvanivaranavishkambhi
5)	Sureshvara	Jambhaka (wk)
6)	Vishvamurtti	Manaka (wk)
7)	Sureshana (Queen Vishvamata)	Khagarbha

Kalki

1)	Yashas (Queen Tara)	Manjughosha (= Manjushri)
2)	Pundarika	Lokanathav (= Avalokiteshvara)
3)	Bhadra	Yamantaka (wk)
4)	Vijaya	Kshitigarbha
5)	Sumitra	Jambhaka (wk)
6)	Raktapani	Sarvanivaranaviskambhi
7)	Vishnugupta	Manaka (wk)
8)	Arkakirtti	Khagarbha
9)	Subhadra	Vighnashakta (wk)
10)	Samudravijaya	Vajrapani
11)	Aja	Yamantaka (wk)
12)	Surya	Kshitigarbha
13)	Vishvarupa	Jambhaka (wk)
14)	Shashiprabha	Sarvanivaranavishkambhi
15)	Ananta	Manaka (wk)
16)	Mahipala	Khagarbha
17)	Shripala	Vighnashakta (wk)
18)	Hari	Vajrapani
19)	Vikrama	Yamantaka (wk)
20)	Mahabala	Kashitigarbha
21)	Aniruddha	Jambhaka (wk)
22)	Narasimha	Sarvanivaranavishkambhi
23)	Maheshvara	Khagarbha
24)	Anantavijaya	Vajrapani
25)	Raudra Chakri	Manjughosha

Kings of the Age of Perfection

1) Brahma (elder son of Raudra Suresha   Manjushri
   (younger son of Raudra, he will rule   Avalokiteshvara
   south of the Sita River, thus he is not
   counted in the dynasty of Shambhala)
2) Kashyapa   a tenth stage bodhisattva
3) Matsya   a bodhisattva emanation
4) Kurma   a bodhisattva emanation
5) Varaha   a bodhisattva emanation
6) Narahari, or Narasimha   a bodhisattva emanation
7) Vamana   a bodhisattva emanation
8) Yamadagni (= Parashurama)   a bodhisattva emanation
9) Rama   a bodhisattva emanation
10) Krshna   a bodhisattva emanation

NOTES

1. Sources: *Nado (S) pp. 1-4, (T) 105/4-106/4; *Sri Kalacakra* (S & T) I. 1-3; Bu ston
    1329:23-27; mKhas grub 1434:129-135; kLong rdol 1765:246-248; Hoffmann
    1973:136-140.

2. Dalai Lama 1981:8.

3. This stupa received its name from an event that occurred during the time of
    Buddha Kanakamuni. There was a bad famine, and a monk magically caused
    a rain of rice to fall for twelve days. This relieved the starving beings. The
    leftover rice was collected and the Heap of Rice (*dhanyakataka*) stupa was
    constructed out of that (kLong rdol 1765:247).

    The Dhanyakataka stupa was located at what is now Amaravati in the
    Guntur District of Andhra Pradesh. Although the stupa was razed by the local
    people for building materials in the 18th and 19th centuries, enough remains
    in the Madras, Calcutta, British, and Amaravati museums to show that it was
    one of the architectural wonders of ancient India. The Dhanyakataka stupa
    dated back to at least the 2nd century A.D., probably earlier.

4. Sources: This section is all translated from kLong rdol 1765:238-246, except
    for the description of the mandala, which is translated from the *Vimalaprabha*
    (S) 15a-15b, (T) 354-355. Cf. also *Sri Kalacakra* (S&T) I. 149-150; mKhas grub
    1434:1068-1079. I have slightly rearranged the order of presentation of kLong
    rdol's narrative. kLong rdol's description of Shambhala is based on the *Kala-
    pavatara* (Peking #5908) and Panchen bLo bzang dpal ldan ye she's *Shambha la'i
    zhing bkod bri tshul* (gSung 'bum "bKa' rgya ma" vol. 13).

    Much ink has been spilled by western scholars speculating about the
    "location" of Shambhala. But so far no one seems to have closely examined
    the Sanskrit Kalachakra texts, the ultimate source of Buddhist Shambhala.
    The Buddhist myth of the Kalkis of Shambhala derives from the Hindu Kalki
    of Shambhala myths contained in the *Mahabharata* and the Puranas. The
    Vimalaprabha even refers to the *Kalkipuranam*, probably the latest of the
    upapuranas. This relationship has been obscured by western scholars who have
    reconstructed the Tibetan translation term *rigs ldan* as "Kulika." Although
    Tibetan *rigs ldan* is used to translate Sanskrit *kulika* in other contexts, here it
    always represents Sanskrit *kalkin* (possessive of *kalkah*; I use the nominative
    kalki). This will be made clear below at the end of the section on Yashas.
    (Western scholars have also falsely reconstructed Yashas's Tibetan name *grags
    pa* as Kirti).

    Although the Buddhist myth of Shambhala derives from the Hindu Kalki
    myth, this does not mean that the Buddhist Shambhala is a mere fiction. If we
    assume a Buddhist Shambhala actually existed at the time of the composition
    of the Sanskrit Kalachakra literature, it is not too difficult to determine what
    historical entity it corresponded to. The primary texts of the Kalachakra
    system came into being around the beginning of the 11th century (see notes 11
    & 13), so Shambhala must have existed at that time. The *Vimalaprabha* tells us
    that Shambhala is on a latitude north of Tibet, Khotan, and China. Further-
    more, the *Vimalaprabha* says again and again that Shambhala is north of the

Sita River. The descriptions of the Chinese traveler, Hsuan tsang (7th century), and the Tibetan traveler, Man lungs Guru (13th century), both clearly identify the Sita as the Tarim River in Eastern Turkistan. Thus, "Sambhala" must be a special name for the Uighur kingdom centered at Khocho that flourished *circa* 850–1250. Needless to say, substantiation of this theory will require another essay. In particular, we will have to consider the entire matrix of the 11th century Asian history together with the motives of the Kalachakra myth-makers.

5. Sources: *Vimalaprabha* (S) 13a-14b, (T) 346–354; Bu ston 1329:27–28; mKhas grub 1434:135–137, 165; kLong rdol 1765:248.

6. Sources: *Vimalaprabha* (S) 14a-17b, (T) 351–361; Bu ston 1329: 53–55; mKhas grub 1434:152, 166; Bandyopadhyaya 1952:74–75. The section between the asterisks is translated from the *Vimalaprabha*.

7. The five psychic powers are clairvoyance, clairaudience, mind reading, remembrance of one's own and others' former existences, and the magical power of flying in space.

8. In general the term *smrti* refers to the whole body of brahmanical sacred literature that is the product of human authors. *Smrti* is contrasted with *shruti* which, strictly speaking, refers only to the mantra sections of the Vedas, that were divinely intuited by the ancient seers. The *smrtis* quoted below are probably taken from the *Brahmanas* or *Dharmashastras*—the Vedic ritual and law textbooks.

9. Vishavimla (*bi si mi lla*): This is the form that appears in the oldest manuscript from which I am working; (mss. do not distinguish *ba* and *va*). Hoffmann (1969:62, 64–65) has proposed that this "mantra of the barbarian deity" repre-sents the Arabic *bismillah*: "in the name of Allah." This can hardly be ques-tioned given the context. The usual name for "the barbarian deity" used in the *Sri Kalacakra* and the *Vimalaprabha* is Rahmana (*rahma na*). This represents the Arabic *al-Rahman*, "the Merciful." See also note 13 below.

10. The five sins of immediate retribution are patricide, matricide, murder of an arhat, intentionally wounding a tathagata, and creating schism in the Sangha. These sins are so heinous that, unless antidotes are employed, their karmic results definitely ripen in the very next life.

11. This statement must be qualified. The *Paramadibuddha* is the basic or root tantra (*mulatantra*) of the Kalachakra system. The *Sekoddesa* (Peking #3) is a section extracted from the fifth chapter of the *Paramadibuddha*, and the *Tantra-garbha* (Peking #6) is a condensation of material drawn from the fourth chap-ter of the *Paramadibuddha*. Also, hundreds of verses quoted from the *Paramadi-buddha* appear in the Indian Kalachakra literature.

    However, the *Paramadibuddha* as a whole has not been preserved in Sanskrit and was not translated into Tibetan. Thus, for the Kalachakra system as a whole the *Sri Kalacakra* functions as the basic tantra for the Tibetans and ourselves.

12. See: *Srivajramalabhidhanamahayogatantra sarvatantrahrdayarahsyavibhanga nama* (the *Vajramala*) Peking #58; vol. 3, 226/1/5; and *Sridvibhujasahajasamvarasadhana* by Shri Vajraghanta Peking #2155; vol. 51, 183/2/1–3. I suspect these verses are interpolated in the preceeding texts; they all appear in the *Vimalaprabha* as well.

13. *Sri Kalacakra* (S & T) I. 27.ab; *Vimalaprabha* (S) 5lb, (T) 480–481. The date is written in "number symbols" (*vahnau khe 'bdhau*) that represent the number 403. Previous Tibetan and western-style scholars have concluded that this year corresponds to the first year of the newer Tibetan chronology, i.e., 1027 A.D. There are some good reasons for accepting this interpretation.

    However, the *Vimalaprabha* explains that this year 403 is "the year of the lord of the barbarians" (*mlecchendravarsham*). Furthermore, the lord of the barbarians is "Muhammad, the incarnation of al-Rahman, the teacher of the barbarian Dharma, the guru and swami of the barbarian Tajiks" (*madhumati rahmanavataro mlecchadharmadeshako mlecchanam tayinam guruh svami*). Given this, it seems to me that the year 403 should be caluculated in the era of the Hijra: 403 A.H. equals 1012–1013 A.D.

14. 'Gos lo tsa ba 1478:672.

15. The text translated below is Bu ston 1329:56–61. mKhas grub 1434:167–173 corresponds verbatim to Bu ston's version of the Rwa tradition, but it differs a little in the 'Bro lineage account. The differences are mainly in the form of additional information, and I have inserted this in my translation. mKhas grub's text was translated by Roerich 1932:18–22. I hope I have improved upon Roerich's generally excellent translation; in any case, the journal it was published in is extremely rare and difficult to obtain.

    Those with an appetite for more stories about the spread of the Kalachakra in India should see 'Gos lo tsa ba 1478:661–673, translated by Roerich 1949:753–766. 'Gos lo tsa ba collected a virtual cornucopia of these legends, and their basic unreliability becomes apparent when they are juxtaposed. This problem is especially pressing for the very beginning of the Kalachakra tradition in India. Any given story of the introduction of the Kalachakra into India can be contradicted by another, equally venerable story. The only way to extract history from such material is to bring in external evidence, as I have tried to do below.

16. For more on the mysterious Shing stan can see Roerich 1949:1021–1022, 1031. The "Sendhapas" were Sinhalese Theravadin monks active in Magadha during the Pala and Sena dynasties. I have collected a number of references to them from the Tibetan histories, and I hope to publish an article on them in the near future.

17. "The One Possessing Power In Ten Aspects" is a mantric cosmogram symbolizing the entire universe as conceived in the Kalachakra. It consists of a number of different-colored letters woven together, and it often appears above the doors and gateways of Tibetan monasteries and temples. The manifesto *Kalachakrapada the Younger wrote over the door of Nalanda is taken

from the *Vimalaprabha* (S) 33b, (T) 419–420. *Namasamgiti* is the short title of the *Manjushrijnanasattvasya-paramarthanamasamgiti* (Peking #2). The *Vimalaprabha* says this short text contains the definitive meaning of all the mantra systems of the Mantrayana.

18. The *Sekoddesa* has been mentioned above (note #11). The *Sekaprakriya* (Peking #7 & 4609) treats the Kalachakra initiation rituals. It is composed of three blocks of verses from the *Sri Kalacakra*, two from the third chapter and one from the fifth. The commentary referred to is probably Darika's **Sri-Kalaca-kratantrarajasya sekaprakriyavrtti vajrapadodghati nama* (Peking #2072).

19. I have adopted the form "Pindo" from 'Gos lo tsa ba 1478:664–666, 671. The references in the rest of this paragraph were first collected by Ruegg 1981:215–218. I am grateful to Ronald M. Davidson for drawing my attention to Ruegg's article.

20. Peking #5343; vol. 103, 21/5/1–4.

21. *Bodhimargapradipapanjika nama* Peking #5344;vol. 103, 44/4/1-45/4/3.

22. Bu ston, Collected Works (cited under Bu ston 1329 in the bibliography), Part 3 (GA), 319.

23. Taranatha 1608:214.

24. My reconstruction of *Nado's Prakrit name is a combination of the Sanskrit form reported by Carelli (see *Nado (S)) and the most common Tibetan form: *Na ro pa*, or *Na ro*. A safe approximation for the date of *Nado's nirvana has been established by Wylie 1982: 687–692.

25. Bu ston 1329:74.

26. The Tibetan histories contain an abundance of generally reliable information on the spread of the Kalachakra in Tibet. What follows is necessarily just a sketch, and it is written from the point of view of the dGe lug pa school. The account through mKhas grub is drawn from Bu ston 1329:61–74; mKhas grub 1434:173–197. For more on the spread of the Kalachakra in Tibet see 'Gos lo tsa ba 1478:673–741, translated by Roerich 1949:766–838.

27. Some recent writers have characterized Bu ston as a kind of enemy of the rNying ma traditions. This is utterly false. Bu ston's biography records his study of rNying ma tantra, including the *rdzogs chen*. Also, Bu ston defended the authenticity of rNying ma tantra translations for which Sanskrit originals could be found.

28. Edited and translated by Schubert 1953:424–473.

29. Edited and translated by Grunwedel 1915.

30. Sources: *Sri Kalacakra* (S & T) I. 151–153, 158–168. (The *Vimalaprabha* does not comment on these verses.) My interpretation of these verses is based on mKhas grub 1434:1082–1091, 1098–1111. Some details are taken from kLong rdol 1765:256–262.

31. Sources: *Sri Kalacakra* (S & T) I. 152, 156–157, 165–167; *Vimalaprabha* (S) 14b-15a, (T) 351–354; mKhas grub 1434:148–151, 436–438, 1096–1098, 1106–1110; kLong rdol 1765: 248–251.

BIBLIOGRAPHY

WORKS IN SANSKRIT AND TIBETAN

Bu ston (1329)
   Bu ston Rin chen grub: *bsDus ba'i rgyud kyi rgyal po dus kyi 'khor lo'i 'grel bshad rtsa ba'i rgyud kyi rjes su 'jug pa stong phrag bcu gnyis pa dri ma med pa'i 'od ces bya ba'i bshad thabs kyi yan lag rnam par gzhag pa rgyud sde rin po che thams cad kyi sgo 'byed par byed pa rin po che gces pa'i lde mig ces bya ba* (a.k.a. *Dus 'khor chos 'byung*). Contained in Lokesh Chandra (ed.), *The Collected Works of Bu-ston* Part 4 (NGA), (New Delhi: International Academy of Indian Culture, 1965), ff. 1–92.

'Gos lo tsa ba (1478)
   'Gos lo tsa ba gZhon nu dpal: *Deb gter sngon po* (*The Blue Annals*). Lokesh Chandra (ed.), (New Delhi: International Academy of Indian Culture, 1976).

mKhas grub (1434)
   mKhas grub dGe legs dpal bzang: *rGyud thams cad kyi rgyal po bcom ldan 'das dpal dus kyi 'khor lo mchog gi dang po'i sangs rgyas kyi rtsa ba'i rgyud las phyung ba bsdus ba'i rgyud kyi 'grel chen rtsa ba'i rgyud kyi rjes su 'jug pa stong phrag bcu gnyis pa dri ma med pa'i 'od kyi rgya cher bshad pa de kho na nyid snang bar byed pa zhes bya ba* (a.k.a. *Dus 'khor tik chen*). Contained in *Yab sras gsung 'bum*, mKhas grub KHA (Dharamsala, Himachal Pradesh, India: Tibetan Cultural Printing Press (Shes rig bar Khang), 1983).

kLong rdol (1765)
   KLong rdol bla ma Ngag dbang blo bzang: *Dang po'i sangs rgyas dpal dus kyi 'khor lo'i lo rgyus dang ming gi rnam grangs*. Contained in Lokesh Chandra (ed.), *The Collected Works of Longdol Lama*, (New Delhi: International Academy of Indian Culture, 1973), ff. 232–282.

*Nado (S)
   Mario E. Carelli (ed.), *Sekoddesatika of Nadapada (Naropa)*, (Baroda, India: Oriental Institute, 1941), Gaekwad's Oriental Series #90.

*Nado (T)
   Paramarthasamgraha nama sekoddesatika, (Peking #2068; vol. 47).

Peking
   Daisetz T. Suzuki (ed.), *The Tibetan Tripitaka* (Peking Edition), (Tokyo-Kyoto: Tibetan Tripitaka Research Institute, 1955 ff.).

Sri Kalacakra (S)
   Paramadibuddhoddhrta Sri Kalacakra nama tantraraja. Contained in Lokesh Chandra (ed.), *Kalacakra tantra and Other Texts*, Part 1, (New Delhi: International Academy of Indian Culture, 1966).

Sri Kalacakra (T)

    mChog gi dang po'i sangs rgyas las phyung ba rgyud kyi rgyal po dpal dus kyi 'khor lo zhes bya ba. Contained in Lokesh Chandra (ed.), *The Collected Works of Bu-ston,* op. cit., Part 1 (KA).

Taranatha (1608)

    rGya gar chos 'byung. Contained in Tseten Dorji (ed.), *Five Historical Works of Taranatha,* (Tibetan Nyingmapa Monastery, Camp No. 5, Lohit, Arunachal Pradesh, India: Tseten Dorji, 1974).

Vimalaprabha (S)

    Vimalaprabha nama mulatantranusarini dvadasasahasrika laghukalcakratantraraja-tika. Film-strip No. MBB-1971-24, (Stony Brook, New York: The Institute for Advanced Studies of World Religions, 1971).

Vimalaprabha (T)

    bsDus ba'i rgyud kyi rgyal po dus kyi 'khor lo'i 'grel bshad rtsa ba'i rgyud kyi rjes su 'jug pa stong phrag bcu gnyis pa dri ma med pa'i 'od ces bya ba. Contained in Lokesh Chandra (ed.), *The Collected Works of Bu-ston,* op. cit., Part 1 (KA)

WORKS IN WESTERN LANGUAGES

Bandyopadhyaya (1952)

    Biswanath Bandyopadhyaya, "A Note on the Kalacakratantra and its Commentary," *Journal of the Asiatic Society Letters,* vol. 18 (1952), pp. 71–76.

Dalai Lama (1981)

    His Holiness the (14th) Dalai Lama, *Concerning the Kalachakra Initiation in America,* (Madison, Wisconsin: Deer Park, 1981).

Grünwedel (1915)

    Albert Grunwedel, "Der Weg nach Sambhala," *Abhandlungen der königlich Bayerischen Akademie der Wissenschaften,* Band 29, 3 (1915).

Hoffmann (1969)

    Helmut Hoffmann, "Kalacakra Studies I: Manichaeism, Christianity, and Islam in the Kalacakra Tantra," *Central Asiatic Journal,* vol. 13 (1969), pp. 52–73.

Hoffmann (1973)

    Helmut Hoffmann, "Buddha's Preaching of the Kalacakra Tantra at the Stupa of Dhanyakataka," *German Scholars on India,* vol. 1, (Varanasi: The Chowkhamba Sanskrit Series Office, 1973), pp. 136–140.

Roerich (1932)

    Georges de Roerich, "Studies in the Kalacakra," *Journal of the 'Urusvati' Himalayan Research Institute of the Roerich Museum,* vol. 2 (1932), pp 11–23.

Roerich (1949)
    George N. Roerich, *The Blue Annals*, (Delhi: Motilal Banarsidass reprint, 1976).

Ruegg (1966)
    D.S. Ruegg, *The Life of Bu ston Rin po che*, (Roma: Istituto Italiano per il Medio
    ed Estremo Oriente, 1966), Serie Orientale Roma XXXIV.

Ruegg (1981)
    D. Seyfort Ruegg, "Deux Problèmes d'Exégèse et de Pratique Tantriques,"
    Michel Strickmann (ed.), *Tantric and Taoist Studies*, vol. 1, pp. 212–226, (Brux-
    elles: Institut Belge des Hautes Études Chinoises, 1981), Melanges Chinois et
    Bouddhiques, vol. XX.

Schubert (1953)
    Johannes Schubert, "Das Wunschgebet um Shambhala," *Mitteilungen des Insti-
    tuts fur Orientforschung*, Band 1 (1953), pp. 424–473.

Wylie (1982)
    Turrell V. Wylie, "Dating the Death of Naropa," L. A. Hercus *et. al.* (ed.),
    Indological and Buddhist Studies, (Delhi: Sri Satguru Publications reprint, 1984),
    pp. 687–692.

THE WHEEL OF TIME

The Kalachakra
Tantra Initiation

GESHE LHUNDUB SOPA[1]

INTRODUCTION

The Kalachakra or "Wheel of Time" (*dus kyi 'khor lo*) is a tantra
that plays a unique and paradoxical role in Tibetan Buddhism. On
the one hand, most Tibetan Buddhists believe it to represent the
very pinnacle of Buddhist esoterism. The Kalachakra presents the
Buddha's most profound and complex statement on matters both
worldly and religious, and its intricacies have placed it beyond the
ken of all but a specialized few scholars and practitioners[2] who can
master it only by understanding a vast range of traditional ideas
and practices. On the other hand, initiations into the meditational
practice of Kalachakra are the only *Anuttara* Yoga tantra initiations
that are offered to the general public. The Kalachakra's association
with the kingdom of Shambhala, the ground of a future revival of
the Dharma, gives it a special eschatological focus.

Presence at a Kalachakra initiation, whose blessings may help
one to be reborn in Shambhala in the future, is considered highly
auspicious. Such initiations, particularly when offered by a Dalai
Lama, usually are attended by thousands upon thousands of the
faithful.[3]

Kalachakra literature has five main subjects: cosmology (*'jig rten gyi khams rnam par bkod pa*), psycho-physiology (*nang nges pa*), initiation (*mngon par dbang bskur ba*), sadhana (*sgrub thabs*) and gnosis (*ye shes*). In an article this brief, not even an outline of these subjects can be presented. Therefore, I will try to expose only a very small part of the Kalachakra tradition, specifically, the seven initiations analogous to events in childhood (*byis pa ltar 'jug gi dbang bdun*). These are the heart of the great public ceremonies just mentioned.

I will briefly place the Kalachakra within the context of Mahayanist—especially tantric—Buddhism, and will sketch the stages of the Kalachakra initiation that precede the actual seven initiations. The bulk of the paper will be a straightforward account of the seven initiations, in whose unfolding we encounter the most fundamental theme of tantra: the transformation of the ordinary into the divine. I will conclude with a few remarks first about the generation stage (*bskyed rim*) sadhana that, having received the seven initiations, one is empowered to practice, and about the initiations and practices of the completion stage (*rdzogs rim*).[4]

(A thorough discussion of the generation stage sadhana will be found elsewhere in this volume.)

KALACHAKRA IN CONTEXT

The Kalachakra teachings appeared in India toward the end of the first millenium A.D. Many modern scholars thus have regarded the Kalachakra as a "late" tantra, and a highly syncretic one, showing Hindu and Central Asian influences. In the traditional view held by most Tibetan Buddhists, the Kalachakra actually was taught by the Buddha during his earthly career in the early to middle part of the first millenium B.C. Thus, its appearance in India a thousand or more years later is actually a *re*appearance, or reintroduction from the land of Shambhala, where it had been kept since the Buddha's time.

Since I am concerned here to place the Kalachakra within the system of those who presently practice and transmit it, I will present the traditional view, without commenting on the many historical problems that either the traditional or "modern" view entails.

According to tradition, the Buddha taught the 12,000-verse *Kala-chakra Mulatantra* at the request of King Suchandra of the Central Asian land of Shambhala. The transmission occurred at the stupa of Shri Dhanyakataka, in south India,[5] where the Buddha also transmitted a number of other tantras, including those of Yaman-taka and Chakrasamvara. Suchandra returned to Shambhala, where he wrote a 60,000-verse on the *Mulatantra*. Seven generations later, Manjushrikirti established the Kalachakra as the main reli-gious system of Shambhala. He wrote a 1000-verse summary of the *Mulatantra* called the *Kalachakra Laghutantra*. His successor, Pun-darika, wrote a 12,000-verse commentary on the *Laghutantra*, the *Vimalaprabha*. When the Kalachakra teachings were returned to India late in the first millenium A.D., only the *Laghutantra* and the *Vimalaprabha* were transmitted. Thus, only those two were trans-lated in their entirety into Tibetan when the Kalachakra system was introduced to Tibet in the eleventh century.[6]

It is generally agreed that the greatest Tibetan scholar of the Kalachakra has been Bu ston (1290–1364), who wrote voluminously on the topic. Other great scholars of the system have included Tsong kha pa's disciple mKhas grub (15th century), the bKa' brgyud pa Pad ma dkar po (15th century) and kLong rdol bla ma (18th century).[7]

As noted above, the fundamental Kalachakra literature is divided into five chapters, covering cosmology, psycho-physiology, initiation, the sadhana of the generation stage, and the gnosis attained by the completion stage. Most later commentators sub-sume these topics under the "three Kalachakras." The first, the Outer Kalachakra (*phyi'i dus 'khor*), deals with the external cosmos and its cycles, through astrology, geography, history and eschatol-ogy. The second, the Inner Kalachakra (*nang gi dus 'khor*), deals with the cycles internal to humans through an analysis of the chakras (*'khor lo*), channels (*rtsa*), winds (*rlung*), drops (*thig le*) and minds (*sems*) that are the basis of tantric psycho-physiology. The third, the Other Kalachakra (*gzhan gyi dus 'khor*), is the generation and com-pletion stage practices that purify the outer and inner Kalachakra, transforming one into a buddha.

In the arrangement of tantras into four categories adopted by most Tibetan *gSar ma pa* traditions, the Kalachakra is considered an

Anuttara Yoga tantra (bla na med pa'i rgyud). *Anuttara* Yoga is the highest level of tantra and the most advanced of all Buddhist meditational systems. Most Tibetan traditions assume that one must practice it in order to attain the unsurpassed, perfect enlightenment of buddhahood. *Anuttara* yoga tantras are divided according to emphasis. Those called "father tantras" emphasize the generation of the illusory body (*sgyu lus*) that is the basis of a buddha's form body. Those called "mother tantras" emphasize the clear light (*'od gsal*) gnosis, or the inseparability of bliss and emptiness that is the basis of a buddha's dharmakaya.

Although some commentators have placed the Kalachakra in a third class called "nondual" tantras, the most authoritative traditions consider it a mother tantra.[8] Like all *anuttara* yoga tantras, the Kalachakra practice is divided into two stages: a generation stage, where the primary concern is with the visualization of oneself as a deity within the context of a mandala; and a completion stage, where the primary concern is with the purification of one's winds and drops within the central channel (*dbu ma*), a process that culminates in one's attainment of buddhahood.

The *Anuttara* Yoga tantra is part of the larger category of practices known as Tantrayana, or Vajrayana. Tantrayana, or the Tantra Vehicle, together with the more "conventional" practices of the Sutrayana, or Paramitayana, the Sutra or the Perfection Vehicle, form the Bodhisattvayana, more commonly known as the Mahayana. The Mahayana or "Greater Vehicle" together with the Hinayana or "Lesser Vehicle" include all possible Buddhist systems.

In the view of the dGe lugs pa school, following the Prasangika Madhyamika system of Chandrakirti,[9] what differentiates the various vehicles is not the object of a wisdom consciousness; that, in all cases is emptiness (*shunyata; stong pa nyid*). Rather, what differentiates the vehicles from each other is the extensivenss of the methods (*upaya; thabs mkhas*) employed in the attainment of one's spiritual goal.

Mahayana, thus, is differentiated from Hinayana by its emphasis on *bodhicitta (byang chub sems)* or the aspiration to attain enlightenment not only for one's own liberation, but for the sake of the liberation of all sentient beings. Within Mahayana, the tantra vehicle is differentiated from the sutra vehicle by its emphasis on the cultivation of advanced samadhis. In these, one "takes the goal as the path" by visualizing oneself as the divinity one will become; one also directly manipulates the channels, winds and drops that are the actual basis of defilement and purification.

Tantric practice is tremendously difficult. It presupposes that one has generated the basic Buddhist renunciation of the suffering of samsara or cyclic existence, as well as having generated both the basic Mahayana motive of *bodhicitta*, and some understanding of wisdom. Just as important as these three, is the willingness—vital to tantric practice—to follow the instructions of one's guru or teacher. In addition to all this, the practice of tantra requires that one be initiated by a qualified master, or vajraguru.

It is on this process of initiation, in the context of the Kalachakra tantra, that the remainder of this article will concentrate.

THE KALACHAKRA INITIATION: PREPARATORY PHASES

Like all tantric initiations (*abhisheka; dbang bskur*) the Kalachakra initiation involves the disciple's entrance into the mandala of the deity in question. There the disciple is empowered by the main deity and other deities to practice various meditations, and these deities plant in the disciple's mindstream the seeds of various supermundane attainments.

Most *Anuttara* Yoga tantra initiations are divided into four: 1. a vase (*kalasha; bum pa*) initiation which is subdivided into water, crown, vajra and bell, and name initiations; 2. a secret (*guhya; gsang ba*) initiation; 3. a wisdom-gnosis (*prajna-jnana; shes rab ye shes*) initiation; 4. a "fourth" (*turiya; bzhi pa*) initiation. Generally, the vase initiation empowers one to practice the generation stage of a particular tantra, while the latter three initiations give the power to practice the completion stage.[10]

The Kalachakra initiation, on the other hand, is divided into eleven initiations. Seven initiations are analogous to events in childhood, specifically, the water, crown, crown pendant, vajra and bell, conduct, name and permission. These together empower the disciple to practice the generation stage. There are then four "conventional worldly" (*kun rdzob 'jig rten pa*) and "transmundane" (*nges don 'jig rten las 'das pa*) higher initiations (*dbang gong ma*) that empower the disciple to practice the completion stage.[11]

These seven initiations analogous to events in childhood just mentioned above, must be given in dependence upon a mandala of colored sand or powder. The construction of such a mandala is a delicate and painstaking process, and the preparatory rituals of the initiation are complex. Thus, although the seven initiations themselves are conferred on a single day, preparations for them may take as many as eleven days. The following is an outline of these preparatory phases.[12]

The very first step in the initiation is a Disciple Ritual (*slob mas gsol ba btab cing bsrung ba bya ba*). During this the disciples, or their representatives, first request that the vajraguru proceed with the initiation; the guru then "plants" the seed-syllable of the tathagatas who head the six tantric "families" (*rigs*) at the disciple's six chakras.

Next come the four Rituals of the Site (*sa'i cho ga*). Testing the Site (*sa brtag pa*) requires gaining assurance that the site is suitable as a place for construction of the mandala.[13] Requesting the Site (*sa bslang ba*) involves obtaining permission for the initiation from both temporal authorities and divine beings. Purifying the Site (*sa sbyang ba*) involves first clearing the area physically, and then purifying it ritually through the creation of a circle of protective deities (*bsrung 'khor*), then, the placement of protective demon-pinning knives (*phur bu*) around the place where the mandala will be, followed by a contemplation of emptiness. Taking the Site (*sa bzung ba*) involves receiving permission from various Tathagatas to create the mandala, and the summoning and dispersal of interfering forces through the elaborate "dance of the site" (*sa gar*).

The Rituals of the Site are followed by the six Rituals of Preparation (*sta gon gyi cho ga*).[14] In the Preparation of the Earth Goddesses (*sa'i lha mo lhag gnas*), flowers and perfume are offered to earth goddesses from the center of the place where the mandala will be; the goddesses are then visualized melting into the offerings. In the Preparation of the Five Substances (*rdzas lnga lhag gnas*), the guru and the assistants consecrate five types of physical things that are to be used in the initiation ritual: vases full of purified water in which deities are generated, the chalk lines to be used for outlining the mandala, the sand particles from which the mandala will be constructed, and the vajra (*rdo rje*) and bell that the guru will use throughout the initiation.

The third of the Rituals of Preparation, the Preparation of the Disciple (*slob ma'i lhag gnas*) will be outlined below. In the fourth ritual, the Preparation of the "Bed" (*mal stan lhag gnas*) the guru and the assistants analyze their dreams to ensure that conditions are propitious for the construction of the mandala. In the Preparation of the Chalk Lines (*las thig lhag gnas*), the guru and the assistants ritually set the four major axes and the four base lines of the mandala, and place a few grains of sand at each point where a deity will be represented. In the Preparation of the Deities (*lha lhag gnas*), the actual deities of the actual Kalachakra mandala are summoned from their abode to descend into the area that has been prepared for the mandala.

The next preparatory phase is the actual construction of the mandala. Construction is preceded by the setting of a five-threaded "gnosis line" on the main outlines of the mandala, and the demarcation of three concentric mandalas of mind, speech and body into which the entire mandala is divided; this is done with sands of the basic color of each (black, red and white respectively).

After the mandala has been completed, it is blessed by the guru. Demon-pinning knives are set around it, as are ten ritual vases. The mandala is further adorned in various ways. Finally a curtain is lowered on all four sides to shield it from the uninitiated, and a celebratory dance of the offering goddesses is performed.

Following the mandala construction, the Preparation of the Disciple is performed. This usually consists of six stages. 1. The guru instructs the disciple on the proper motivation for receiving initiation, and on *bodhicitta*—the altruistic aspiration to enlightenment. Then the guru leads the disciples through an "inner initiation" (*nang gi dbang*); this is a spiritual "rebirth" that empowers them to visualize themselves as Kalachakra in union with his consort, Vishvamata. 2. The disciples formally request initiation from the guru, who assents by silence, and then promises to reveal the path to enlightenment. 3. The disciples take the bodhisattva and tantric vows.[15] The guru then blesses the body, speech and mind of each disciple by touching each of them with a conch containing consecrated water. 4. Each disciple casts a "toothstick" (*so shing*) onto a small mandala to determine which of the tathagata lineages she or he is most closely identified. The guru gives each disciple consecrated water for three purificatory sips, and then presents each of them with a red protection string along with two sheaves of kusha grass to be used in analyzing dreams. 5. The disciple visualizes at each of the six chakras the six syllables *oM, ah, huM, ho, haM,,* and *ksah* that will be the basis of the transformation of each disciple's mundane elements into the gnosis of the tathagatas. The guru requests Vajrasattva to initiate the disciples and to aid their spiritual efforts. 6. The guru urges the disciples to renounce samsara or cyclic existence, and to generate enthusiasm for tantric practice. Finally, the guru instructs the disciples on dream examination.

The next day, the last of the preparatory rituals before the actual conferral of the seven initiations is performed. This centers on the disciple's entering into the mandala. It begins with the guru commenting on the meanings of dreams that the disciples may have had the previous night. The guru then recites the requirements for both the tantric master and the tantric disciples. The disciples formally request admission to the mandala. Some disciples now are given deity costumes to wear, to aid in visualizing themselves as Kalachakra/Vishvamata. All disciples receive a blindfold that they are to put on immediately, and a dried flower that will be offered later.

After re-establishing their divine identity as Kalachakra/Vishvamata—which is also the form in which they must constantly see the guru—the disciples again take the bodhisattva and tantric vows, adding to the latter specific pledges directed to each of the tathagatas. After the guru has ritually stabilized the disciples' *bodhicitta,* the mandala is revealed to them. At its center is a four-faced, twenty-four armed Kalachakra, in union with a four-faced, eight-armed Vishvamata. Each disciple visualizes herself or himself circumambulating the mandala, prostrating to each of Kalachakra's four faces; for each prostration, the disciple transforms into the tathagata corresponding to the particular face.

After the guru urges them to maintain secrecy about the initiation, the disciples absorb the actual deities or gnosis beings (*jnanasattva; ye shes pa*) inhabiting the mandala into themselves. Finally, each of the disciples offers the dried flower to the main deity by dropping it onto a small mandala. The disciple receives a tantric name, and then is instructed to remove the blindfold and view the interior of the mandala.

The mandala of Kalachakra contains 722 deities. The outermost, the body mandala (*sku'i dkyil 'khor*) contains 536 deities, most of whom are elemental and calendrical. Enclosed within the body mandala is the speech mandala (*gsung dkyil 'khor*) which contains 116 deities including a large number of speech *yoginis* (*rnal 'byor ma*). Finally, enclosed within that is the mind mandala (*thugs dkyil 'khor*) with 70 deities, including Kalachakra/Vishvamata, as well as shaktis or power beings (*nus ma*), tathagatas, bodhisattvas and protectors. The deities from the mind mandala are the ones who actually confer the seven initiations.

THE SEVEN INITIATIONS[16]

As already noted, the seven initiations empower the disciple to practice the generation stage of the Kalachakra tantra. In each of the initiations, the disciple takes the form of a particular tathagata. Each initiation involves the transformation of both external and internal substances. Each one empowers the disciple to attain certain spiritual goals, and each is analogous to a particular event in the development of a child.

THE WATER (*Chu*) INITIATION[16]

Standing at the eastern door of the mandala, the disciple visualizes the guru, in the form of Kalachakra/Vishvamata, approaching the disciple and holding out his vajra. Taking one end of the vajra, the disciple is led clockwise around the mandala to the northern door. There the disciple sees Kalachakra's left, white face; this face symbolizes the purification of body. After the disciple offers a mandala and requests the water initiation, rays shine out from the *hum* at Kalachakra's heart. These rays draw the disciple into the diety's mouth, down his central channel, through the "vajra path" and into the "lotus" of Vishvamata. The disciple melts into a drop, which dissolves into emptiness. From emptiness emerges an *om* that becomes a lotus; the lotus becomes a white, three-faced, six-armed Amitabha,[17] in union with a red, three-faced, six-armed Pandara.[18]

Rays from the *huM* at Kalachakra's heart draw down the gnosis beings and the initiatory deities, male and female bodhisattvas and their consorts. The initiation deities ignite the fire of desire at Kalachakra's heart. The fire melts the *bodhicitta*/white drop substance at his crown. The *bodhicitta* flows down the central channel and into the lotus/womb of Vishvamata, where it confers "inner" initiation upon the disciple. The disciple emerges from Vishvamata's lotus and sits on the initiation seat at the northern door, in the form of Amitabha/Pandara.

The transformation of the substances of the initiation into deities occurs next. In the water initiation, the external substance is the water contained by the ten vases that encircle the mandala. The internal substances are the disciple's five "ordinary" elements ('byung ba), that correspond to the upper five chakras. The initiatory deities into which the substances are transformed are the consorts of the five tathagatas.

The disciple visualizes the five elements and vase water dissolving into emptiness. The space element and water from the conch and the upper and lower vases become an *ah* that becomes a vajra; this becomes a green, three-faced, six-armed Vajradhatvishvari, in union with a blue, three-faced, six-armed Vajrasattva. (All the deities generated from the substances have three faces and six arms.) The disciple's wind element and water from the conch and the east and southeast vases become a long *i* that becomes a sword; this becomes a black Tara, in union with a yellow Vairocana. The disciple's fire element and water from the conch and the south and southwest vases become a long vocalic *R* that becomes a jewel; this becomes a red Pandara, in union with a white Amitabha. The disciple's water element and water from the conch and the north and northeast vases become a long *u* that becomes a lotus; this becomes a white Mamaki, in union with a red Ratnasambhava. The disciple's earth element and water from the conch and the west and northwest vases become a long vocalic *L* that becomes a wheel; this becomes a yellow Locana, in union with a black Amoghasiddhi. These deities, and all subsequent initiatory deities as well, are marked with an *oM* at the forehead, an *ah* at the throat, a *huM* at the heart, and a *hoh* at the navel.

From the *huM* at each deity's heart come light rays, which draw down the gnosis beings corresponding to the "pledge beings" (dam tsig pa) just generated. The gnosis beings melt into the pledge beings, and initiation goddesses confer initiation upon the deities. Each consort's initiation is sealed at the crown by the head of her tathagata lineage. The twelve offering goddesses make offerings for the enjoyment of the senses. Then, from the heat of their union with their tathagatas, the consorts melt into the water that is the external substance of the initiation.

Rays from Kalachakra's heart rouse the initiatory male and female bodhisattvas; offerings and a request for initiation are made to them. The buddhas and bodhisattvas indicate that they will grant initiation. At this indication, the bodhisattvas make auspicious gestures, while offering goddesses make offerings, flowers rain from the sky, and wrathful deities expel hindrances. Then, the five consorts confer initiation by touching the conch to the disciple's "five places," i.e. the crown of the head, both shoulders and both thighs. In order to be purified, the disciple is sprinkled with water and given some to taste.

At the moment of initiation, here, and in all subsequent initiations, the disciple feels that the inner substance has been made serviceable. The disciple generates a non-conceptual wisdom; this wisdom becomes bliss, and this culminates in a state of awareness in which bliss and wisdom are inseparable. There follows a verse celebrating the auspiciousness of the initiation.

Finally, there is a follow-up "water" initiation. The disciple visualizes the space element as Vajradhatvishvari at the crown chakra, the wind element as Tara at the forehead, the fire element as Pandara at the throat, the water element as Mamaki at the heart, and the earth element as Locana at the navel. Doubles emerge from the actual consorts in the mind mandala and melt into the disciple's elements. Initiatory buddhas and bodhisattvas are summoned. They too melt into the disciple's elements, transforming them into the five consorts.

This completes the water initiation. The water initiation has purified the disciple's five elements, empowered the disciple to win the attainments of the five consorts, and reach the first bodhisattva stage (*bhumi; sa*). It is said to be analogous to an infant's first bath after birth.

THE CROWN (*Cod pa*) INITIATION

Still sitting as Amitabha on the initiation seat outside the northern door of the mandala/mansion, the disciple makes the offering
of the entire universe by visualizing it—this is the mandala offering—and then requests the crown initiation. The external substance of the crown initiation is a five-segmented crown, each
segment of which has a different color corresponding to each of
the five tathagata lineages as they appear in this tantra. The internal substances are the disciple's five ordinary aggregates (skandha;
phung po). The initiatory deities into which the five aggregates are
transformed are the five tathagatas with their consorts.

The disciple visualizes the five aggregates and the five crown
segments dissolving into emptiness. The consciousness aggregate
and the green crown segment become an *a*; this becomes a vajra
and this becomes a green, three-faced, six-armed Akshobhya in
union with a blue, three-faced, six-armed Prajnaparamita. The disciple's formation aggregate and the black crown segment become
an *I*; this becomes a sword and this becomes a black Amoghasiddhi
in union with a yellow Locana. The disciple's feeling aggregate and
the red crown segment become a vocalic *R*; this becomes a jewel
and this becomes a red Ratnasambhava in union with a white
Mamaki. The disciple's perception aggregate and the white crown
segment become an *u*; this becomes a lotus and this becomes a
white Amitabha in union with a red Pandara. The disciple's form
aggregate and the yellow crown segment become a vocalic *L*; this
becomes a wheel, and this becomes a yellow Vairocana in union
with a black Tara.

As before, the generated deities draw down their corresponding gnosis beings, and initiation goddesses confer initiations. The
initiations are sealed by the heads of the tathagata lineages. Offerings are made, and the tathagatas, from the heat of union with their
consorts, melt into the crown that is the external substance of the
initiation.

A sequence of requests is then made to the initiatory deities.
The five tathagatas then confer initiation by touching the crown to
the disciple's five places. In the follow-up water initiation, the disciple visualizes the consciousness aggregate at the crown as
Akshobhya, the collection aggregate at the forehead as Amogha-

siddhi, the feeling aggregate at the throat as Ratnasambhava, the perception aggregate at the heart as Amitabha, and the form aggregate at the navel as Vairocana. As before, doubles from the actual deities in the mind mandala,[20] as well as initiatory buddhas and bodhisattvas, melt into the disciple, transforming the aggregates into the five tathagatas.

This completes the crown initiation. This initiation has purified the disciple's five aggregates. The disciple is empowered to win attainments of the five tathagatas, and also to reach the second bodhisattva stage. It is said to be analogous to a child's first haircut.

The first two initations are held at the northern door of the mandala/mansion. Upon completion of these two, the disciple has laid the basis for purifying the elements, aggregates and the drop at the forehead chakra, as well as for achieving the adamantine body (*sku'i rdo rje*) of an enlightened being.

THE CROWN PENDANT (*Dar dpyangs*) INITIATION

At the northern gate, the guru again proffers his vajra, and leads the disciple clockwise around the mandala to the southern door. There the disciple confronts Kalachakra's right, red face; this face corresponds to the purification of speech. The disciple offers a mandala and requests the crown pendant initiation. Once again, the disciple is drawn into Kalachakra's mouth and down into the lotus of Vishvamata; there the disciple undergoes inner initiation and emerges as a red, three-faced, six-armed Ratnasambhava in union with a white, three-faced, six-armed Mamaki. In this form, the disciple sits on the initiation seat at the southern door.

The external substances of the crown pendant initiation are the ten parts of the crown pendant. The internal substances are the ten principal winds that course through the body. The initiatory deities into which the substances are transformed are the ten shaktis who embody the ten perfections (*paramitas; pha rol tu phyin pa*) of Mahayana Buddhism.

The disciple visualizes his or her ten winds and the crown pendant dissolving into emptiness. As in the Crown Initiation, and in all subsequent initiations, there will be generation of deities from the initiation substances. In this initiation, the deities generated from the first four sets of substances all have four faces and eight arms.

The disciple's equally-abiding and "turtle" winds and the two black parts of the pendant become an *a* and a *ha*; these become a censer and a black yak-tail fan, and these become the east shakti, a black four-faced, eight-armed Krishnadipta, and the southeast shakti, a black four-faced, eight-armed Dhuma. The disciple's upward-moving and "lizard" winds and the two red parts of the pendant become an *ah* and a *hah*; these become a butter lamp and a red yak-tail fan, and these become the south shakti, a red Rakta-dipta and the southwest shakti, a red Marici. The disciple's perva-sive and "god-given" (*devadatta*) winds and the two white parts of the pendant become an *aM* and a *haM*; these become ambrosia and a white yak-tail fan, and these become the north shakti, a white Shvetadipta and the northeast shakti, a white Kadayota. The disci-ple's "serpent" and "fire" (*dhananjaya*) winds and the two yellow segments of the pendant become an *a* and a *ha*; these become a conch and a yellow yak-tail fan, and these become the west shakti, a yellow Pitadipta and the northwest shakti, a yellow Pratipa. The disciple's vitalizing wind and the green segment of the pendant become a *ho*; this becomes a vajra, and this becomes a green, three-faced, six-armed Vajradhatvishvari. The disciple's down-voiding wind and the blue segment of the pendant become a *phreM*; this becomes a curved knife and this becomes a blue, three-faced, six-armed Vishvamata.

As before, the generated deities draw down their correspond-ing gnosis beings, and the initiation goddesses confer initiations that are sealed by Vajrasattva. Offerings are made, and the shaktis melt into the crown pendant that is the external substance of the initiation.

Again, a sequence of requests is made to the initiatory deities. Then the ten shaktis confer initiation by touching the crown pen-dant to the disciple's five places and draping the pendant over the crown so that it hangs down on either side of the disciple's head.

In the follow-up water initiation, the disciple visualizes eight winds as eight shaktis on the eight "petals" or sections of the "lotus" at the heart chakra, and then visualizes the ninth, vitalizing, and the tenth, downward-voiding winds as shaktis that are transfor-mations of the disciple's three upper and three lower main channels respectively. As before, doubles from the actual deities in the mind mandala, that is, the eight shaktis surrounding Kalachakra/ Vishvamata and the two "contained" in Vishvamata, as well as the initiatory buddhas and bodhisattvas, melt into the disciple, thus tranforming the disciple's winds into the ten shaktis.

This completes the crown pendant initiation. It has purified the disciple's ten winds. The disciple is empowered to win attainments of the ten shaktis, to complete the ten perfections, and to reach the third bodhisattva stage. It is analogous to the ear-piercing and the first adornment of a child.

THE VAJRA AND BELL (rDo rje dril bu) INITIATION

Still sitting on the initiation seat outside the mandala's southern door as Ratnasambhava, the disciple offers a mandala and requests the vajra and bell initiation. The external substances of the vajra and bell initiation are a vajra and a bell. The internal substances are the disciple's right and left channels. The initiatory deities into which the substances are transformed are Kalachakra and Vishvamata.

The disciple visualizes the channels and the vajra and bell dissolving into emptiness. The disciple's right channel and the vajra become a *huM*; this becomes a vajra, and this becomes a "simple" or one-faced, two-armed black Kalachakra, in union with a yellow Vishvamata. The disciple's left channel and the bell become a *phreM*; this becomes a curved knife, and this becomes a simple yellow Vishvamata, in union with a black Kalachakra.

As before, the generated deities draw down their corresponding gnosis beings, and the initiation goddesses confer initiations. Kalachakra's initiation is sealed by Akshobhya; Vishvamata's initiation is sealed by Vajrasattva. Offerings are made and, from the heat of union with their consorts, Kalachakra and Vishvamata melt respectively into the vajra and bell that are the external substances of the initiation.

A sequence of requests is made to the initiatory deities. Kalachakra and Vishvamata confer initiation by touching the vajra and bell to the disciple's five places. The guru rings the bell, at which point the disciple imagines that the initiation has been received.

In the follow-up water initiation, the disciple visualizes the right and left channels as Kalachakra and Vishvamata respectively. As before, doubles from the actual deities in the mind mandala, as well as initiatory buddhas and bodhisattvas, melt into the disciple, thus transforming the right and left channel into Kalachakra and Vishvamata.

This completes the vajra and bell initiation. It has purified the disciple's right and left channels. The disciple is empowered to concentrate winds from the right and left channels in the central channel, to gain the indestructible bliss and exalted non-conceptual wisdom of Kalachakra and Vishvamata and to reach the fourth bodhisattva stage. With the completion of the third and fourth initiations, held at the southern door of the mandala, the disciple has laid the basis for purifying the winds, channels, and the drop at the throat chakra, as well as for achieving the adamantine speech (*gsung rdo rje*) of an enlightened being.

THE VAJRA CONDUCT (*rDo rje brtul zhugs*) INITIATION

At the southern gate, the guru again proffers his vajra, and leads the disciple clockwise around the mandala to the eastern door. Here the disciple confronts Kalachakra's front, black face; this face corresponds to the purification of mind. The disciple offers a mandala and requests the vajra conduct initiation. Once again, the disciple is drawn into Kalachakra's mouth and down into the lotus of Vishvamata. There the disciple undergoes inner initiation and emerges as a black, three-faced, six-armed Amoghasiddhi, in union with a yellow, three-faced, six-armed Locana. In this form, the disciple sits on the initiation seat at the eastern door.

The external substance of the varja conduct initiation is a vajra thumb ring, symbolic of engaging objects with a mind that combines bliss and gnosis. The internal substances are the six organs, that is, the five sense organs and the mental organ, and the objects of those organs. The initiatory deities into which the substances are transformed are the six male and six female bodhisattvas.

The disciple visualizes the sense organs and sense objects and the ring dissolving into emptiness. The disciple's ear and the mental objects and the ring become an *a* and a long *a*; these become vajras, and these become a green, three-faced, six-armed Vajrapani in union with a blue, three-faced, six-armed Shabdavajra, and also a green, three-faced, six-armed Dharmadhatuvajra in union with a blue, three-faced, six-armed Samantabhadra. The disciple's nose and tangibles and the ring become an *e* and an *ai*; these become swords, and these become a black Khagarbha in union with a yellow Gandhavajra, as well as a black Sparshavajra in union with a yellow Sarvanivaranavishkambhi. The disciple's eye and taste objects and the ring become a vocalic *R* and a long vocalic *R*; these become jewels, and these become a red Kshitigarbha in union with a white Rupavajra, as well as a red Rasavajra in union with a white Lokeshvara. The disciple's tongue and forms and the ring become an *o* and an *au*; these become lotuses, and these become a white Lokeshvara in union with a red Rasavajra, as well as a white Rupa-vajra in union with a red Kshitigarbha. The disciple's body and all odors and the ring become a vocalic *L* and a long vocalic *L*; these become wheels, and these become a yellow Sarvanivarana-vishkambhi in union with a black Sparshavajra, as well as a yellow Gandhavajra in union with a black Khagarbha. The disciple's mental organ and sounds and the ring become a nasal *M* and an *ah*; these become vajras, and these become a blue Samantabhadra in union with a green Dharmadhatuvajra, as well as a blue Shabda-vajra in union with a green Vajrapani.

As before, the generated deities draw down their correspond-ing gnosis beings, and initiation goddesses confer initiations which are sealed by the heads of the lineages. Offerings are made and, from the heat of union with their consorts, the male and female bodhisattvas melt into the thumb ring that is the external substance of the initiation.

The sequence of requests is made to the initiatory deities. The male and female bodhisattvas confer initiation by touching the ring to the disciple's five places and placing it on the disciple's thumb.

In the follow-up water initiation, the disciple visualizes the organs and objects as the six male and six female bodhisattvas, respectively. As before, doubles from the actual deities in the mind mandala, as well as initiatory buddhas and bodhisattvas, melts into the disciple, transforming the organs and their objects into the male and female bodhisattvas.

This completes the vajra conduct initation. It has purified the disciple's organs and their objects. The disciple is empowered to have proper conduct, and to use objects without attachment, and with full recognition of their ultimate emptiness and their status as the "sport" of blissful gnosis. The initiation further empowers the disciple to win attainments of the bodhisattvas and to gain the fifth bodhisattva stage. It is analogous to a child's first enjoyment of mental and sense objects.

THE NAME (*Ming*) INITIATION

Still sitting on the initiation seat outside the mandala's eastern door as Amoghasiddhi, the disciple offers and mandala and requests the name, or bracelet (*gdub bu*) initiation. The external substance of the name initiation is a bracelet, symbolic of behavioral restraint. The internal substances are various bodily parts and their functions. The initiatory deities into which the substances are transformed are the six male and six female wrathful deities who guard the directions in the mind mandala.

The disciple visualizes the bodily parts and functions and the bracelet dissolving into emptiness. The disciple's urinary organ, and the act of ejaculation, and the bracelet become a *ha* and a long *ha*; these become vajras, and these become a green, three-faced, six-armed Ushnishachakravarti in union with a blue, three-faced, six-armed Atinila, as well as a green, three-faced, six-armed Raudrakshi in union with a blue, three-faced, six-armed Sumbharaja. The disciple's mouth, the act of defecation, and the bracelet become a *ya* and a long *ya*; these become swords, and these become a black Vignantaka in union with a yellow Stambhaki, as well as a black Atibala in union with a yellow Yamantaka. The disciple's arms, the act of going, and the bracelet become a *ra* and a long *ra*; these become jewels, and these become a red Prajnantaka in union with a white Mamaki, as well as a red Jambhaki in union with a white Padmantaka. The disciple's legs, the act of grasping, and the bracelet become a *va* and a long *va*; these become lotuses, and these become a white Padmantaka in union with a red Jambhaki, as well as a white Mamaki in union with a red Prajnantaka. The disciple's defecatory organ, the act of speaking, and the bracelet become a *la* and a long *la*; these become wheels, and these become a yellow Yamantaka in union with a black Atibala, as well as a yellow Stambhaki in union with a black Vignantaka. The disciple's "supreme" or sexual organ, the act of urination, and the bracelet become a *haM* and a *hah*; these become vajras, and these become a blue Sumbharaja in union with a green Raudrakshi, as well as a blue Atinila in union with a green Ushnishachakravarti.

As before, the generated deities draw down their corresponding gnosis beings, and the initiation goddesses confer initiations which are sealed by the heads of the lineages. Offerings are made and, from the heat of union with their consorts, the male and female wrathful deities melt into the bracelets that are the external substances of the initiation.

The sequence of requests is made to the initiatory deities, the male and female wrathful deities confer initiation by touching the bracelet to the disciple's five places and by placing it on the disciple's wrists.

After the main part of the initiation, the guru stands on his seat, holding his robes in a "leonine" manner to indicate fearlessness. He proceeds to prophesy the disciples' attainment of enlightenment under the various tantric names they have assumed on entering the mandala, each name corresponding to one of the five tathagatas. The disciples are told that when the guru utters the appropriate name, they are to generate nonconceptual wisdom; this wisdom becomes bliss and this culminates in a state of mind where bliss and wisdom are inseparable. The guru further prophesies that all the disciples eventually will attain identity with Varjasattva, the embodiment of the inseparability of bliss and gnosis, and put an end to cyclic existence.

In the follow-up water initiation, the disciple visualizes the body parts and functions as the male and female wrathful deities. As before, doubles from the actual deities in the mind mandala, as well as initiatory buddhas and bodhisattvas, melt into the disciple, transforming the body parts and functions into the male and female wrathful deities.

This completes the name initiation. It has purified the disciple's body parts and functions, and empowered the disciple to win attainments of the wrathful deities and destroy evil forces through the power of the four immeasurables. The four immeasurables are love, compassion, sympathetic joy and equanimity. It also empowers the disciple to reach the sixth bodhisattva stage. The name initiation is analogous to the naming of a child.

With the completion of the fifth and sixth initiations, held at the eastern door of the mandala, the disciple has laid the basis for purifying the organs and their objects, for purifying the body parts and their functions, as well as the drop at the heart. These two initiations are said to lay the basis for achieving the adamantine mind (*thugs rdo rje*) of an enlightened being.

THE PERMISSION (*rJes gnang*) AND ITS ANCILLARIES

The last of the seven initiations is the permission. This is divided into the actual permission and it ancillaries. The actual permission begins at the eastern gate. The guru again proffers his vajra, and leads the disciple clockwise around the mandala to the western door. There the disciple confronts Kalachakra's rear, yellow face; this corresponds to the purification of gnosis. The disciple offers a mandala and requests the permission. Once again the disciple is drawn into Kalachakra's mouth and down into the lotus of Vishvamata where he or she undergoes initiation and emerges as a yellow, three-faced, six-armed Vairocana, in union with a black, three-faced, six-armed Tara. In this form the disciple sits on the initiation seat at the western door.

The external substances of the actual permission are the symbols of the five tathagatas: a vajra for Akshobhya, a sword for Amoghasiddhi, a jewel for Ratnasambhava, a lotus for Amitabha, and a wheel for Vairocana. The internal substances are the gnosis aggregate and the consciousness element.[21] The initiatory deities into which the substances are transformed are Vajrasattva and Prajnaparamita, together with their consorts.

The disciple visualizes the gnosis aggregate and the consciousness element and the five symbols dissolving into emptiness. The internal and external substances emerge from emptiness and become a *haM* and a *kshah*; these become vajras, and these become a blue, three-faced, six-armed Vajrasattva in union with a green Dharmadhatvishvari, as well as a blue, three-faced, six-armed Prajnaparamita in union with a green Akshobhya.

As before, the generated deities draw down their corresponding gnosis beings, and initiation goddesses confer initiations; these are sealed by Akshobhya. Offerings are made and, from the heat of union with their consorts, Vajrasattva and Prajnaparamita melt into the five symbols that are the external substances of the initiation.

The sequence of requests is made to the initiatory deities. Vajrasattva and Prajnaparamita confer initiation by touching the five symbols to the disciple's five places, after which the disciple is to generate an awareness in which bliss and gnosis are inseparable.

In the follow-up water initiation, the disciple visualizes the bliss aggregate as Vajrasattva and the consciousness element as Prajnaparamita. As before, doubles from the actual deities in the mind mandala[22] as well as initiatory buddhas and bodhisattvas melt into the disciple; the disciple's bliss aggregate and consciousness element are transformed into Vajrasattva and Prajnaparamita.

In the last ritual of the actual permission, the disciple takes a wheel as the seat, lays a sacred text across his or her knees, and holds a conch in the right hand and a bell in the left. The disciple rings the bell while reciting verses that express the intention to work for the welfare of others in accordance with each individual's particular needs and spiritual lineage.

The first ancillary of the permission is the transmission of mantras. The disciple, in the form of Kalachakra/Vishvamata, visualizes each mantra at the guru/deity's heart, circling the *huM* there. As the guru utters the mantra, its syllables emerge from his mouth. When the disciple utters the mantra for the first time, the mantra enters and surrounds the *huM* at the disciple's heart. With the second repetition, the mantra becomes undifferentiable from the disciple's own identity as Kalachakra. With the third repetition, the mantra becomes firm. The most important mantra transmitted is the "essence" mantra of Kalachakra: *oM ah huM ho haM kshah ma la va ra ya huM phat.*

In the second ancillary, the guru gives the disciple three substances: a spoonful of eye medicine that symbolically clears away obstacles to the conceptual realization of emptiness; a mirror that helps the disciple to view all phenomena as empty and like a reflection; and a bow and arrow that symbolizes the "penetration" of object by subject in a direct, non-conceptual realization of emptiness.

The last, and most important, ancillary of the permission is the initiation of the vajra guru. The external substances of this initiation are a vajra and bell. The internal substance is one's body as a whole. The deities into which the substances are transformed are Vajrasattva and Prajnaparamita. The disciple reduces herself or himself and the vajra and bell to emptiness. The disciple and the vajra become a *huM*; this becomes a vajra, and this becomes a blue, three-faced, six-armed Vajrasattva, in union with Dharmadhat-vishvari. The disciple and the bell become an *ah*; this becomes a curved knife, and this becomes a blue, three-faced, six-armed Prajnaparamita, in union with Akshobhya. The generated deities draw down their corresponding gnosis beings, and the initiation goddesses confer initiations; these are sealed by Akshobhya. From the heat of union with their consorts, Vajrasattva and Prajnaparamita melt into the vajra and bell that are the external substances of the initiation. The guru places a vajra in the disciple's right hand and a bell in the disciple's left. With crossed hands, the disciple thinks that bliss, (the vajra), and gnosis, (the bell), have been generated simultaneously, and that in virtue of this simultaneous generation of bliss and gnosis, she or he has become identified with Vajrasattva.

The guru then imparts to the disciple a set of instructions that seem to contradict conventional morality. Those disciples of the vajra-Akshobhya lineage are told to kill; those of the sword-Amoghasiddhi lineage are told to lie; those of the jewel-Ratnasambhava lineage are told to steal; those of the lotus-Amitabha lineage are told to commit adultery; those of the wheel-Vairocana lineage are told to drink alcohol; those of the curved knife-Vajrasattva lineage are told to not deride the "sky lotus" or womb of females. Each of these instructions is merely a symbolic way of talking about aspects of tantric practice. For example, the advice to kill means that the disciple should stop the vital downward flow of *bodhicitta* substance and the ten "emission" winds.

With the completion of the permission initiation, the last of the seven initiations is completed. The permission initiation, held at the western door of the mandala, has purified the disciple's bliss aggregate and consciousness element. The disciple is empowered to attain the adamantine gnosis (*ye she rdo rje*) inseparable from emptiness that is the nature of Vajrasattva. The disciple is empowered to purify the drop at the navel, and to reach the seventh bodhisattva stage. It is said to be analogous to a child's first reading lesson.

POST-INITIATION RITUALS

After the completion of the seven initiations analogous to events in childhood, there are a number of concluding ceremonies. The guru announces the particulars of the time when the initation has been granted, that is, the year of the Buddhist era, on which day in which astrological month in which year in the reign of which king of Shambhala, etc. The guru then gives the disciples various instructions on practice, in particular urging their observance of the tantric vows.

The final ceremony is the dismantling of the mandala: the sands from which the mandala was constructed are swept to the center of the mandala area, placed in an ornamented vase, and taken to a river or lake where the resident nagas are propitiated and the sand ceremoniously returned to its original source.

THE GENERATION AND COMPLETION STAGES

There is no room here for a detailed description of the generation and completion stage practices empowered by the Kalachakra initiations. However, I will simply outline them here to round out this brief account of the Kalachakra system.

The generation stage sadhana begins with the instantaneous generation of oneself as Kalachakra/Vishvamata. This is followed by inner offerings and offerings to one's self-generation. One recites the hundred-syllable mantra of Vajrasattva, and then recites certain lines to increase one's stores of merit and gnosis. Then one creates a protection wheel of wrathful deities.

The actual sadhana of the generation stage is divided into four parts.
1. The supreme victorious mandala (*dkyil 'khor rgyal mchog*) entails the generation of Kalachakra/Vishvamata surrounded by eight

shaktis from the letter *haM* that is the mingling of wind, mind, and the white and red drops. This is followed by the generation of the remaining deities of the mandala from the lotus/womb of Vishvamata.

2. The supreme victorious activity (*las kyi rgyal mchog*) entails the dissolution and regeneration of the central couple, followed by the absorption of the mandala deities into Kalachakra's crown and their regeneration from the lotus/womb of Vishvamata. Then, the five wrathful protectors are drawn down, and one grants all deities the seven initiations; these are sealed by the heads of the tathagata lineages.

3. The yoga of the drops (*thig le'i rnal 'byor*) entails the experience of the "four joys" (*dga' ba bzhi*) as the white drop, melted by the heat of the main couple's sexual union, passes from Kalachakra's crown to the tip of his "vajra" or penis.

4. The subtle yoga (*phra mo'i rnal 'byor*) entails the even deeper experience of the four joys as the white drop is drawn back up the central channel to the crown.[23]

The completion stage, empowered by the four "conventional worldly" and "transmundane" higher initiations,[24] is divided into six yogas whose purpose is one's enlightenment as an "empty form" (*stong gzugs*) analogous to the illusory body produced in the completion stage of other *anuttara* yoga tantras.[25]

1. In the yoga of withdrawal (*so sor sdud*), one dissolves one's winds into the central channel and generates at one's forehead chakra a small semblance of the empty form of Kalachakra/Vishvamata.

2. In the yoga of stabilization (*bsam gtan*), one concentrates on the empty form with the divine pride that one *is* that empty form.

3. In the yoga of breath control (*srog bsdud*), one moves the empty form to the navel chakra, and uses vajra-recitation and vase breathing to bring the vitalizing and downward-voiding winds together there. The winds ignite the inner fire (*gtum mo*), and this melts the white drop at the forehead; the melted drop moves down the central, and this results in the experience of the four joys.

4. In the yoga of retention (*'dzin pa*), the drop moves back up the central channel, and one experiences the four joys as a basis for the realization of the inseparability of bliss and gnosis.

5. In the yoga of mindfulness (*rjes dran*), one generates an actual empty form at the navel, and then uses a real or visualized consort

(*mudra; phyag rgya*) to generate great bliss through stabilizing the white drop at the tip of the "vajra" and the red drop at the crown. 6. In the yoga of samadhi (*ting nge 'dzin*), one stacks in the central channel the 21,600 white or male drops and the 21,600 red or female drops. The stacking of each drop entails an experience of bliss and the cutting off of one of the winds that are the basis of cyclic existence. When all the drops have been stacked, one is enlightened, or a buddha in the empty form aspect of Kalachakra/ Vishvamata.[26]

NOTES

1. I would like to thank Dr. Roger Jackson for assistance in the preparation of this article. This was originally prepared for presentation at the Sixth Conference of the International Association of Buddhist Studies (Tokyo-Kyoto, 1983).

2. It is not, for instance, a main subject of study at either of the principal dGe lugs pa (Gelugpa) tantric colleges, rGyud stod (Gyodto) and rGyud med (Gyud me). In Tibet, it traditionally was a specialty of the Panchen Lama and the monks of bKra shis lhun po (Tashilunpo). Its traditions are still carried on by the monks of rNam rgyal grwa trshang (Namgyal trasang), the small college, now located in Dharamsala, India, affiliated with the Dalai Lama.

3. The present, fourteenth Dalai Lama has offered the Kalachakra initiation three times just in the last decade: in 1974, in Bodh Gaya, India, in 1976, in Leh, India, and in 1981, in Madison, Wisconsin, U.S.

4. Reserved for more advanced and specialized practitioners, completion stage initiations seldom are given at large public initiations. The latter almost invariably are limited to the seven initiations analogous to events in childhood. These empower only the generation stage practices.

5. It has been indentified by many scholars with the Amaravati stupa, in present-day Andhra Pradesh, India.

6. The Tibetan translation of the *Laghutantra* is found in *Kalachakra Tantra and Other Texts*, ed. Raghu Vira and Lokesh Chandra, vol. 69 in Sata Pitaka Series (New Delhi: International Academy of Indian Culture, 1966). The *Vimalaprabha*'s Tibetan translation is no. 2064 in *Tibetan Tripitaka, Peking Edition*, ed. Daisetz T. Suzuki (Tokyo: Tibetan Tripitaka Research Institute, 1957), vol, 46. Both are extant in Sanskrit.

7. The *gsung 'bum* of these various scholars may be consulted for their works on the Kalachakra.

8. For a discussion of this issue, see *Introduction to the Buddhist Tantric Systems*, A. Wayman and F. D. Lessing's translation and edition of mKhas grub rje's *rGyud sde spyi'i rnam par gzhag pa rgyas par brjod* (Delhi: Motilal Banarsidass, 1978) pp. 250–267.

9. As set forth in the first chapter of his *Madhyamakavatara*, which is not extant in Sanskrit, but whose Tibetan version has been edited and partially translated by Louis de la Vallee Poussin.

10. For a discussion of these four initiations, see Wayman and Lessing, chapter nine.

11. The "four" are figured as followed: 1. the worldly and transmundane vase initiations; 2. the worldly and transmundane secret initiations; 3. the worldly and transmundane wisdom-gnosis initiations, together with the fourth initiation; 4. the transmundane fourth initiation.

12. My main source for this section is the *bCom ldan 'das dpal dang po'i sangs rgyas dus kyi 'khor lo'i dbang chen gtsal skabs nyer mkho'i zin bris dwangs gsal me long* (Dharamsala, n.p., n.d.). This is the handbook used by the monks of rNam rgyal grwa tshang (Namgyal Tratsang). Cf. also Wayman and Lessing, chapter eight, and the *Kalachakra Initiation* (Madison: Deer Park, 1981).

13. This procedure can be replaced by a purificatory reading of a prajnaparamita sutra.

14. Other texts count anywhere from four to eight Rituals of Preparation, although the same elements are found in all.

15. Bodhisattva vows can be either the simple promise to attain enlightenment for the sake of all beings, or eighteen root and forty-six auxiliary vows that make the pledge specific. There are fourteen root and eight secondary tantric vows. All the above vows are listed in *Kalachakra Initiation*, pp. 74–76.

16. My account of the seven initiations is based chiefly on the ritual text of the initiation, *Dus 'khor dbang chog nag 'gros su bkod pa*, woodblock print (n.p., n.d.).

17. The color attributed to each deity is that of his/her body and main face.

18. Note that the placement and colors of the tathagatas is different here from the Akshobhya mandala, for example. The Akshobhya mandala is the basis for the Guhyasamaja and Chakrasamvara tantras. Cf., e.g., Alex Wayman, *Yoga of the Guhyasamaja Tantra* (Delhi: Motilal Banarsidass, 1977), pp. 126–136.

19. Vajradhatvishvari is not actually represented in the mandala, but is "contained" in Kalachakra.

20. Akshobhya is not actually represented in the mandala, but is "contained" in Kalachakra.

21. The five "ordinary" aggregates and elements were the internal substances transformed, during the second and first initiations respectively.

22. Vajrasattva and Prajnaparamita are not actually represented in the mandala, but are "contained" in Kalachakra and Vishvamata.

23. For a clear summary of the generation stage, cf. kLong rdol bla ma, *Dang po'i sangs rgyas dpal dus kyi 'khor lo'i lo rgyus dang ming gi rnam grangs*, in *The Collected Works of Longdol Lama*, ed. Lokesh Chandra (New Delhi: International Academy of Indian Culture, 1973), pp. 270–275.

24. For a brief account of them, cf. dGe 'dun grub (Gendun Drub) *Bridging the Sutras and Tantras*, tr. Glenn H. Mullin (Valois, NY: Gabriel/Snow Lion, 1981) pp. 122–123.

25. The empty form differs from an illusory body chiefly in that it is not based on subtle winds, but is, rather, mentally created. Cf. Gendun Drub, pp. 138–140.

26. For a more detailed account of the six yogas, cf. Gendun Drub, pp. 129–155.

The Kalachakra Generation–Stage Sadhana

ROGER JACKSON

INTRODUCTION

The word *sadhana* derives from a Sanskrit verbal root that means "to accomplish" or "to achieve." *Sadhana* itself can denote the accomplishment of a particular aim, goal or object, or it can denote the *means* of accomplishing it. The religious usage of *sadhana* most closely approximates this instrumental sense. In this usage, a sadhana is a text and/or practice that serves as a means for accomplishing a particular religious goal. The Tibetan translation of *sadhana, sgrub thabs,* makes this explicit: *thabs* is a method for accomplishing *sgrub.*

Used religiously, *sadhana* generally refers to a tantric medita-tional procedure, a method for achieving identification with a deity. In the Buddhist tantras, permission to practice the sadhana of a particular deity is conferred through an initiation or cere-mony of permission.

In *Anuttara* Yoga tantra, the highest of the four classes of tantra, *sadhana* generally refers to the practices of the generation stage (*utpattikrama; bskyed rim*), whereby one mentally creates the man-dala-abode of the deity, imagines oneself as the deity at its center,

and populates the mandala with various other deities. The meditations of the generation stage are preparatory to those of the completion stage (*sampannakrama; rdzogs rim*) whereby one manipulates
one's winds and drops within the subtle body so as to attain the
actual form and dharma bodies of the deity who is a buddha.

In the Kalachakra tantric system, the identification of sadhana
with the generation stage is explicit: the chapter in the *Laghutantra*
that deals with the generation stage is entitled *Sadhana*. In most
Anuttara Yoga tantras, the first of the four initiations, the vase
initiation, empowers one to practice the generation stage sadhana.
In the Kalachakra, it is the seven initiations analogous to events in
childhood, described in the last chapter, that provide the empowerment. Kalachakra sadhanas are of varying lengths and may differ in
orientation. For instance, some sadhanas place the Kalachakra
practice within that of guru or six-session yoga. Here, we will
describe briefly what might be called the "standard" sadhana, containing preparatory offerings and meditations, the creation of a
protective circle, the generation of a mandala and its resident
deities, the absorption of actual deities of "gnosis beings" (*jnanasattva; ye shes pa*) into the imagined deities or "pledge beings"
(*samayasattva; dam tshig pa*), the repetition of mantras, etc.

PREPARATORY PRACTICES

Practices preparatory to the "actual sadhana" are divided into
the accumulation of the two stores and the generation of the protective circle. The accumulation of the two stores is itself divided
into preparations and the actual accumulations.

Initially, one generates oneself as a simple blue Kalachakra,
holding crossed vajra and bell, embracing Vishvamata. One then
proceeds to make the inner offering. In the space before one, *yaM*
generates a wind mandala, atop which *raM* generates a fire mandala, atop which *ah* generates a tripod of severed heads, atop which
oM generates a skull-cup. In the skull-cup is an eight-petalled red
lotus, which is marked by the five "nectars"—semen, marrow,
blood, urine and feces—and the five "meats"—elephant, cow,
horse, dog and human. Rays from the *huM* at one's heart stir the
wind, which ignites the fire; the fire melts the substances, and then

the melted substances are stirred from above by a vajra which then melts into them as a moon disc. On a moon in one's left palm is an *oM*, the actual vajra-body; this emits rays that draw down from the vajra-body deities actual nectars that merge with the imagined nectars in the skull-cup, thus purifying them. On a sun in one's right palm is an *ah*, the actual vajra-speech; this emits rays that draw down from vajra-speech deities actual nectars that merge with the imagined nectars, thus making them luscious. On a *Rahu* in both palms is a *huM*, the actual vajra-mind; this emits rays that draw down from vajra-mind deities actual nectars that merge with the imagined nectars, thus setting them aglow. On a *Kalagni* in both palms is a *ho*, the actual vajra-gnosis; this emits rays that draw down from vajra-gnosis deities actual nectars that merge with the imagined nectars, thus turning them all into gnosis nectars.

Next comes the blessing of the vajra and bell. Out of emptiness, come *huM* and a vajra; these become a blue, three-faced, six-armed Vajrasattva, in union with a green Vajradhatvishvari. *ah* and a curved knife become a blue Vishvamata in union with a green Akshobhya. As before, the deities have an *oM* at the forehead, *ah* at the throat, *huM* at the heart, and *hoh* at the navel. Rays from the *huM* at the deity's heart invite down the gnosis beings who, upon the repetition of the phrase *jah huM baM hoh hi*, merge with the pledge beings, i.e., the imagined deities. Rays from each deity's heart-*huM* next draw down the five female tathagatas, who confer initiation with nectar-water. The initiations are crown-sealed, and Vajrasattva and Vishvamata are offered perfume, flowers, incense, light, etc., by the twelve offering goddesses. From the heat of union with their consorts, Vajrasattva and Vishvamata melt into the essence of great bliss, from which they become a vajra and bell respectively.

Now the offerings are blessed. Interferences are dispelled with mantras. In the remaining emptiness are the multiple letters *sphaM*; each letter becomes a great jeweled crystal vessel. The first letter of the name of each offering-substance melts into a vessel, and becomes offerings and offering goddesses, whose nature is emptiness and bliss. As each goddess repeats her offering mantra, one experiences uncontaminated great bliss. Then, one offers the mandala of Mt. Meru, the four continents, etc. The mandala in Kalachakra is arranged somewhat differently than in other practices.

There follows the Vajrasattva recitation. One takes refuge and generates *bodhicitta*, the mind-to-enlightenment. Then, an *oM* at one's crown becomes a white lotus, in which *raM* becomes a sun disc. On the disc, a *kshah* and vajra become a blue Vajrasattva, and an *ah* and vajra become his consort, a green Vajradhatvishvari. Rays from Kalachakra's heart-*huM* draw down the gnosis beings, and these merge with the pledge beings. As before, rays then draw down the five female tathagatas, who confer initiation. Then, the initiations are sealed by the heads of each of the lineages, and the twelve offering goddesses make offerings.

One asks Vajrasattva to purify the evils and broken commitments of oneself and of all sentient beings. Rays from his heart effect this purification. One repeats Vajrasattva's hundred-syllable mantra, and asks his forgiveness for all one's broken vows. He declares them purified, and then melts into one, so that one's body, speech and mind are indivisible from Vajrasattva. This ends the preparations for the accumulation of the two stores.

The actual accumulation of the two stores, namely, merit and gnosis, begins with one's instantaneous self-generation as a simple Kalachakra. A *paM* at one's heart becomes a red lotus, in the center of which is an *oM*; the *oM* becomes a moon-disc, on which is a *huM* and it becomes a vajra. The vajra emits rays drawing down deities into a Kalachakra mandala that is in the space before one, and light rays then melt into the vajra and moon at one's heart.

One then offers a seven-limbed puja. In the first limb, one bows to Kalachakra. In the second, there appears at one's heart the various sets of consonants in sequence; these transform into the various sets of offering goddesses who, with the repetition of mantras, make offerings to please the buddhas, bodhisattvas and protectors. Then, in the third, one confesses one's own transgressions. In the fourth, one rejoices at the virtuous deeds of others. In the fifth, one requests the buddhas to turn the Dharma-wheel. In the sixth, one entreats them not to enter final nirvana or liberation. Finally, in the seventh, one asks the buddhas' aid in dedicating all one's virtue to the attainment of enlightenment for the sake of others.

Upon completion of the seven limbs, one promises henceforth to generate *bodhicitta*, the mind-to-enlightenment, as well as to abandon self-grasping, and to practice the ten perfections (*paramitas*); these ten are the "usual" six plus method, aspiration, strength and gnosis. One expresses love, compassion, sympathetic joy and equanimity for all beings. One promises to abandon the ten non-virtues, the five obstacles, the four defilements that are the root of cyclic existence, and the four contaminants. With the promise to accomplish the "four gates of liberations"—emptiness, signlessness, wishlessness and non-production—one completes the accumulation of the store of merit.

The accumulation of the store of gnosis consists of the repetition of a brief verse reminding oneself that all phenomena are empty of inherent existence. This is followed by a contemplation of emptiness.

The next preparatory practice, the creation of the protective circle, has extensive, middling and condensed versions. Here, we will summarize the extensive version.

There are three main divisions of the protective circle practice: protection of oneself, protection of the place, and follow-up practices.

Protection of oneself begins with the cleansing of body, speech, mind and gnosis. One recites purificatory mantras, then visualizes at one's crown a *vaM* that becomes a sixty-part moon-disc. The moon melts down through one's body three times, and thus one's body becomes white like a moon disc. One then recites the mantra affirming that all dharmas and oneself are naturally pure. Next, one establishes within oneself the six tathagata lineages: an *oM* at one's forehead becomes a white, three-faced, six-armed Amitabha; an *ah* at one's throat becomes a red Ratnasambhava; a *huM* at one's heart becomes a black Amoghasiddhi; a *hoh* at one's navel becomes a yellow Vairocana; a *haM* at one's crown becomes a green Akshobhya; and a *kshah* at one's secret place becomes a blue Vajrasattva.

The third step in protection of oneself is the purification of body, speech, mind and gnosis. One symbolically washes one's hands, reciting purificatory and obstacle-dispelling mantras. Then, various vowels at the bottom, middle and tips of one's left fingers become a fifteen-part moon-disc, and vowels on one's right fingers become a fifteen-part sun-disc. One joins one's palms, and where the moon and sun meet there is a blue *huM*; this, along with the moon and sun, becomes a five-pointed vajra. One blesses one's limbs through various mudras and mantras, then identifies oneself with the nature of all the tathagatas, and holds proudly to this identity.

The fourth step in the protection of oneself is the establishment of one's six limbs. Mantras set at one's heart, head, crown, limbs and two eyes help establish their adamantine nature, and one imagines that one is protected by adamantine armor and weapons.

The final step in protection of oneself is the destruction of demons. One's chakras and each part of one's body are marked by syllables; these transform into vajras with varying numbers of points. When all parts of the body have been thus affected, one thinks that one has attained an adamantine body. The vajras emit variously-colored rays in the ten directions, destroying the demons and hindrances that afflict sentient beings.

The protection of the place consists of the generation of the habitat and the generation of the inhabitants. The generation of the habitat begins with the generation of a triangular space mandala, atop which is a crescent-shaped wind mandala, atop which is a triangular fire mandala. The mandalas merge, and atop them one generates the protective circle's fences and mansion. The outer fivefold fence circles the horizon. The threefold inner fence is set in closer. The fences are set with spears and arrows, and the vast ground they enclose is adamantine in nature.

At the center of the circles is a great mansion, in the middle of which is a sun on a variegated lotus, the seat of Vajravega, the protector-aspect of Kalachakra. Then, moving from the mansion outward, the groups of protectors are established as follows: spaces inside the mansion are allotted to the ten wrathful protectors; spaces just outside the mansion are allotted to the ten depletion deities; spaces inside the threefold inner fence are allotted to the ten direction protectors; spaces outside it are allotted to the ten planetary deities; spaces inside the fivefold outer fence are allotted to the ten nagas; spaces outside it are allotted to the ten elementals.

The generation of the inhabitants begins with generating oneself as Vajravega, Kalachakra's wrathful aspect, atop the sun-disc at the center of the lotus at the center of the mansion. Like Kalachakra, Vajravega is dark blue in body color, with four faces and twenty-four arms. He has no consort, and his faces are uniformly wrathful. After generating oneself in his bodily form, one repeats various mantras, and from various seed syllables Vajravega's various ornaments and hand implements are generated; these ornaments and implements are all adamantine and pure in nature.

Next, from the sun-disc at the heart of oneself as Vajravega, one generates the sixty deities of the protective circle, and sets each in the appropriate place. First, one generates from seed syllables the ten wrathful protectors: Ushnisha, Shumbha, Sarvanivarana-vishkambhi, Niladanda, Prajnantaka, Takki, Padmantaka, Achala, Yamantaka, and Mahabala; they are set within the mansion. Second, one generates the ten "depletion" deities, two deities each representing the depletion, or consumption, of space, air fire, water and earth; they are set outside the mansion. Third, one generates the ten direction protectors: Brahma, Vishnu, Nairrti, Vayu, Yama, Agni, Samudra, Rudra, Indra, and Yaksha; they are set inside the threefold circle. Fourth, one generates the ten planetary deities: Rahu, Kalagni, Moon, Sun, Mercury, Mars, Venus, Jupiter, Ketu and Saturn; they are set outside the threefold circle. Fifth, one generates the ten nagas: Raja, Vijaya, Karkotaka, Padma, Vasuki, Sankhapala, Ananta, Kulika, Mahapadma and Takshaka; they are set inside the fivefold circle. Finally, one generates the ten elementals: a zombie, a vampire, a dog-faced kinnara, a raven-faced kinnara, a pig-faced gandharva, a vulture-faced elemental, a tiger-faced rakshasa, an owl-faced preta, a jackal-faced forgetfulness demon and a garuda; they are set outside the fivefold circle.

Once the pledge beings have been generated and placed in the appropriate spots in the protective circle, the gnosis beings are invoked from their abodes. In the heart of oneself generated as Vajravega, there appears another Vajravega, terrifying in aspect, who sends forth vajra hooks to draw down the gnosis beings; having done this, the vajra hooks then melt back into one's heart. Drawn forth by mantras and mudras, the gnosis being of each of the sixty protective deities descends and becomes of "one taste" with the respective pledge being. Next, one blesses body, speech and mind: body by setting a white *oM* on a moon disc arisen from an *a* at the forehead, speech by setting a red *ah* on a sun disc arisen from a *raM* at the throat, mind by setting a black *huM* on a *Rahu* disc arisen from a drop at the heart. Then, with rays from the *huM* at the heart, oneself and the other deities summon the various initiation deities and request each of the eleven initiations with the appropriate mantra. The appropriate deities then confer each initiation on each protective deity, and the head of each deity's lineage seals the initiations at the crown.

With the completion of the process of generating the inhabitants of the protective circle, one visualizes various mantras circling at one's heart, then repeats them. Their effect is to invoke various deities to dispel the demons and hindrances that afflict beings; to secure the various directions, spheres of existence and aspects of the person; to put to use the various adamantine weapons at one's disposal; and to invoke the aid of the vajra dakinis. At the conclusion of the recitation, one identifies oneself with the tathagatas, the twelve offering goddesses make offerings, and one praises the principal deities.

The last phase of the practices preparatory to the actual sadhana is a follow-up *torma* offering. Still in the form of Vajravega, one consecrates the meat, liquor, water and other offerings; one contemplates emptiness; finally one makes an inner offering, as above. Then one invokes the sixty protective deities: in each case a *haM* at one's gesturing hands becomes a lotus and sun disc, on which is a *hi*; this becomes the symbol of one of the tathagata lineages. The symbols radiate light, and this draws down the deities.

One then offers the ritual cake, *torma*, to each of the deities, repeating mantras that name them, and, as before, one praises the principal deities. Finally, the deities of the protective circle melt into one's respective chakras: the wrathful protectors into a *haM* at one's secret place, the depletion deities into an *oM* at one's crown, the direction guardians into an *i* at one's forehead, the planetary deities into an *R* at one's throat, the nagas into an *u* at one's heart, and the elementals into an *L* at one's navel.

THE ACTUAL SADHANA

The actual sadhana of Kalachakra is divided into four principal parts, or limbs: a. the Supreme Victorious Mandala; b. the Supreme Victorious Activity; c. The Yoga of the Drops; d. the Subtle Yoga. The practice of these four is preceded by the accumulation of the two stores of merit and gnosis, and followed by the repetition of mantras, the making of offerings and praises, the absorption of the mandala deities, and the integration of the practice into one's everyday life.

The preliminary accumulation of the two stores proceeds much as it did before the generation of the protective circle. One accumulates the store of merit through generating oneself as a simple Kalachakra, drawing gnosis beings down into a mandala imagined in front, then directing toward the deities of that mandala the seven-limbed puja, the four immeasurables, and promises to abandon various negativities and achieve various spiritual attainments.

One accumulates the store of gnosis first by reciting a verse that reminds oneself of the emptiness of both meditation and its objects, then by successively dissolving one's elements into emptiness, and finally by reciting mantras that identify one with the "four gates" to liberations: emptiness, signlessness, wishlessness and non-production. This accumulation of the store of gnosis within the sadhana recapitulates the death process undergone by beings in the course of their cyclic transmigration, and is a symbolic preparation for the actual conquest of death, effected on the completion stage.

THE SUPREME VICTORIOUS MANDALA (*dKyil 'khor rgyal mchog*)

The first limb of the actual sadhana, the Supreme Victorious Mandala, entails the preliminary generation of the mandala or "residence" of Kalachakra, and of the deities, or "residents" of the mandala. This is known as the limb of "approximation," and is said to lay the basis for the attainment of the adamantine body of Kalachakra.

The generation of the mandala begins with a triangle symbolic of infinite space; this is often identified with emptiness. Atop that is a black bow-shaped wind "mandala" and atop that are, in ascending order, a red triangular fire mandala, a white circular water mandala, and a yellow square earth mandala. Atop the earth is an adamantine Mt. Meru, at whose summit is a variegated lotus, in which a *haM* becomes moon, sun, *Rahu* and *Kalagni* seats or discs. All that has just been visualized combines into a *haM-kshah-ma-la-va-*

ra-ya letter from which again are generated space, wind, fire, water, earth, Meru, the lotus, and the moon, sun, *Rahu* and *Kalagni* seats. Supported by all of those is a *huM*; this transforms into an adamantine pavilion. Within the pavilion, a *bhruM* transforms into the concentric mind, speech and body mandalas of Kalachakra. The mind mandala is central and highest. The speech mandala is outside the mind mandala, lower, and twice its size. The body mandala, outside the speech mandala and lower still, is twice the size of the speech mandala.

Each mandala has four gates, and is divided into quadrants whose principal colors are black for the east quadrant, red for the south, yellow for the west, and white for the north. Each mandala contains multifarious ornaments, subsidiary animals and symbols, and appropriate seats, pedestals or ledges for the resident deities. Outside the body mandala are circles of earth, water, fire and air, and outside of these is a space circle with a vajra chain fence. Lastly, surrounding the entire construction, is a ring of multi-colored lights.

The first stage in the generation of the mandala's resident deities is the creation of the deities of the mandala's central "circle of great bliss" through the five "enlightenings" (*abhisambodhi; mngon par byang chub pa*). 1. At the center of the mandala, atop the moon-sun-*Rahu*-*Kalagni* seats, is a full moon upon which circle the thirty-two vowels of the Sanskrit alphabet. The moon symbolizes the male drop or *bodhicitta* at the time of a being's conception, and is of the nature of the mirror-like gnosis; the thirty-two vowels are the major marks of a great being. 2. Below the moon is a sun disc, on which circle the eighty consonants. The sun symbolizes the female drop at conception, and is the gnosis of equality; the eighty consonants are the eighty minor marks of a great being. 3. On the moon is a *huM*; this symbolizes the rebirth-consciousness at conception, and is the discriminating gnosis. 4. Marking the moon is a black *hi*; this symbolizes the wind that is the mount of the rebirth consciousness, and is the all-accomplishing gnosis. 5. These four mingle and become a *haM*, which is the gnosis of the dharmadhatu.

The *haM* transforms in Kalachakra, who has four faces, twenty-four arms and two legs. His torso is blue. His front face is black, the right red, the rear yellow and the left white. Each head wears a quintuple crown; his hair is in a yogin's topknot. His two main arms are black and the hands, crossed in front of him, hold a vajra and bell. He has eight black, eight red and eight white arms, each of whose hands holds a particular ritual implement or weapon. His right leg is red and, outstretched, it tramples on Kama, the god of desire. His left leg is white and, drawn in slightly, it tramples on Rudra, the god of wrath. But for gold and diamond ornaments and a loose tiger-skin skirt, he is naked.

Then, a syllable *phreM* transforms into Vishvamata, in sexual union with Kalachakra. She is yellow. Her front face is yellow, the right white, the rear blue and the left red. She has eight arms. The two main arms, around Kalachakra's neck, hold a curved knife and skull-cup; the others hold various implements. Her left leg is outstretched, her right drawn in. Then, on the petals of the lotus on which Kalachakra and Vishvamata stand, various syllables and implements become the eight shaktis, whose colors vary by direction, but each of whom has four faces and eight arms, and is in a pose of "balancing," with one leg on the ground, the other drawn up.

The sound of sexual delight from Kalachakra and Vishvamata now attract Akshobhya and other mind-mandala deities, who take the form of deities of one's aggregates, elements and sense-fields, and melt into Kalachakra's/one's own aggregates, elements and sense-fields. The deities then radiate from Kalachakra's body and permeate Vishvamata. The deities radiate from Vishvamata, and enter Kalachakra's crown. They ignite the fire of desire at his heart, which melts the white drop at his crown. The drop descends through his central channel and passes through his vajra/penis into the lotus/womb of Vishvamata. There, each of the mandala's 722 deities is generated: a drop becomes a seed-syllable, and this becomes a hand symbol; the hand symbol becomes the complete body of the deity, who is then sent forth from the lotus/womb of Vishvamata to take his or her appropriate place in the mandala.

Thus are generated the six male and female tathagatas together with their consorts, the six male and female bodhisattvas and their consorts, and the six wrathful protectors and their consorts, all in the mind mandala; the speech yoginis and other deities of the speech mandala; and the calendrical gods, nagas, cemetery-dwellers and various elementals of the body mandala.

Once the mandala's residents have been set, there emanate

from Kalachakra's/one's own heart rays of light that draw countless
sentient beings down into the mandala. Then, rays from one's heart
draw down the tathagatas and their consorts, who melt into one's
heart. Kalachakra's/one's sexual union ignites the fire of great
desire at the heart. That melts the white *bodhicitta* drop at the
crown, and it flows down the central channel and radiates toward
sentient beings. It bestows initiation on them, and they are filled
with delight, their countenances brightened, their elements, aggregates, organs, objects, limbs and actions transformed into deities.
One concludes the Supreme Victorious Mandala by reciting a
mantra that strengthens one's divine pride by affirming one's identity with the pure dharmadhatu.

THE SUPREME VICTORIOUS ACTIVITY (*Las kyi rgyal mchog*)

The second limb of the sadhana, the Supreme Victorious Activity, entails a regeneration of the mandala deities, the absorption
into them of their corresponding gnosis beings, their initiation by
initiation deities, the blessing of their body, speech and mind, and
a contemplation of the essential purity of the mandala and its
inhabitants. It is known as the limb of approximating accomplishment, and is said to lay the basis for the attainment of the adamantine speech of Kalachakra.

The Supreme Victorious Activity begins with one's own/Kala-
chakra's experience of great bliss, the heat of which causes the
central couple and the eight shaktis to melt into a single drop
whose nature is great bliss. Then there appear four goddesses,
whose nature is that of the four immeasurables. Each, in turn,
exhorts one to take form again for the sake of sentient beings.
Awakened by the goddesses' songs, one beholds the three spheres
of existence clairvoyantly. The moon-lake drop into which one has
melted becomes a radiant blue *huM*; this becomes a vajra, and this
transforms into Kalachakra. Vishvamata is generated in union with
him, and the eight shaktis appear on the lotus petals around the
central couple. All the deities are arrayed as before.

The sound of the sexual delight of Kalachakra and Vishvamata
draws back the host of mandala deities, who enter at Kalachakra's
crown and ignite the fire of desire at his heart. The fire melts the

bodhicitta drop at his crown, and it descends his central channel and enters the lotus/womb of Vishvamata. There it becomes the seed-syllable, then the hand-symbol, then the actual form of each mandala deity. As before, each generated deity goes forth from Vishva-mata and takes his or her proper place in the mandala.

Next, from a *huM* and vajra at one's heart, one generates Vajravega, the wrathful aspect of Kalachakra. With adamantine hooks and weapons, Vajravega draws before one the gnosis beings corresponding to the pledge beings that have been imagined. Vajravega melts back into one's heart, and after offerings, mantras and mudras, one imagines that five wrathful protectors, corre-sponding to one's organs of activity, are summoned, absorbed and bound, made to delight, and made of "one taste" with oneself. Then, the gnosis beings are absorbed into and become of "one taste" with all the deities of the mandala: Kalachakra/Vishvamata, the eight shaktis, the male and female tathagatas, the male and female bodhisattvas, the male and female wrathful protectors, the speech yoginis, the calendrical deities, the nagas, and other minor deities.

Then, light rays from the *huM* at one's heart draw before one all the initiatory deities. With appropriate mantras, one requests each of the eleven initiations, and with appropriate mantras the initiatory deities confer the initiations on all the deities of the mandala. The initiations are imagined to have purified one's defile-ments and propensities to defilement. Then, each deity is "crown-sealed" by the head of his or her lineage. Kalachakra is sealed by Akshobhya, Vishvamata and the eight shaktis by Vajrasattva, deities whose principal color is black by Amoghasiddhi, red deities by Ratnasambhava, white deities by Amitabha, yellow deities by Vairo-cana, blue deities by Vajrasattva and green deities by Akshobhya. In addition, Kalachakra and the six tathagatas are given crowns to wear.

One then seals one's body, speech, mind and gnosis. Body is sealed by an Akshobhya at the crown, an Amoghasiddhi at the heart, an Amitabha at the forehead, a Vairocana at the navel, a Ratnasambhava at the throat, and a Vajrasattva at the secret place. Speech is sealed by an *L* at the navel, an *u* at the heart, an *R* at the throat, an *i* at the forehead and an *ah* at the crown. Mind is sealed by an *oM* at the forehead, an *ah* at the throat and a *huM* at the heart.

Gnosis is sealed by an *a* at the "tip of the adamantine jewel"/penis.

Next, one obtains blessings for one's body, speech and mind. From one's forehead is generated a white vajra-body deity, with three faces and six arms. The vajra-body deity goes forth, teaches the Dharma to sentient beings, and returns to the space before one. One requests initiation from this deity, and goddesses of the body-lineage fill one with nectar, chanting mantras. The vajra-body deity is then absorbed into one's forehead, and one chants verses requesting the blessings of vajra-body. This same sequence is repeated, with appropriate variations, with vajra-speech, a red deity generated from the throat chakra; vajra-mind, a blue deity generated from the heart chakra; and host of vajra-body, vajra-speech, and vajra-mind deities generated from the navel, secret and crown chakras.

The final phase of the Supreme Victorious Activity is the repetition of verses that celebrate the purity of both the residence and residents of the Kalachakra mandala. In celebrating the latter, one notes the symbolic connections between the deities' various attributes and the Outer Kalachakra of the cosmos, the Inner Kalachakra of the body, and the Other Kalachakra of a being transformed by enlightenment.

THE YOGA OF THE DROPS (*Thig le'i rnal 'byor*)

The third limb of the sadhana, the Yoga of the Drops, entails the experience of the four joys, (*ananda; dga' ba*), through the descent through the body of the *bodhicitta* drop. It is known as the limb of accomplishment, and is said to lay the basis for the attainment of the adamantine mind of Kalachakra.

In the Yoga of the Drops, one first visualizes at Kalachakra's and Vishvamata's foreheads an *oM*, at their throats an *ah*, at their hearts a *huM*, at their navels a *hoh*, at their secret place a *haM*, and at their crowns a long *ha*. A *huM* at Kalachakra's secret place transforms into a five-pointed vajra, and his penis-opening is blocked by a *phat*. An *ah* at Vishvamata's secret place transforms into a red lotus, and her vaginal opening is also blocked by a *phat*. Through the force of one's/Kalachakra's contemplation of one's adamantine nature, or— alternatively, through the force of one's sexual embrace—the down-voiding wind ignites the "stainless lightning-like" inner fire at one's navel. The fire's heat rises through the central channel. Its rays descend the left and right channels, purifying the winds associated with the aggregates and elements, and making one's organs impervious to motion or distraction. When the rays strike a *haM* at one's crown, the *haM* melts into a drop, which begins to descend through one's central channel. When it reaches the throat chakra, one experiences joy. When it reaches the heart chakra, one experiences supreme joy. When it reaches the navel chakra, one experiences special joy. When it reaches the jewel-tip at the end of one's "vajra," where the opening is blocked by *phat*, one experiences simultaneous joy, in which bliss and emptiness are cognized simultaneously, and the mandala and the world are as the play of blissful gnosis. This concludes the Yoga of the Drops.

THE SUBTLE YOGA (*Phra mo'i rnal 'byor*)

The fourth limb of the main part of the sadhana, the Subtle Yoga, entails the experience of the four joys through the ascent of the *bodhicitta* drop from the tip of the vajra back to the crown chakra. It is known as the limb of great accomplishment, and is said to lay the basis for the attainment of the adamantine gnosis of Kalachakra.

The Subtle Yoga begins when the drop at the jewel-tip begins to move back up the central channel. When it reaches the navel chakra, one experiences "the result similar to the cause," joy. When it reaches the heart chakra, one experiences "the ripened result," supreme joy. When it reaches the throat chakra, one experiences "the human-made," special joy. When it reaches the crown chakra, one experiences "the separate result," simultaneous joy.

The four "reverse-order" joys of Subtle Yoga *all* presuppose the cognition of bliss and emptiness attained with the simultaneous joy of the Yoga of the Drops. Each joy is more intense than that preceding it. When one experiences the simultaneous joy of the Subtle Yoga, and the drop once again is at one's crown, one's joy is practically limitless, and one's capacity to experience it practically uninterrupted.

The mind that simultaneously experiences bliss and cognizes

emptiness is considered the most powerful of all spiritual forces, because this is the mind free from all gross defilements and dualistic appearances, and also because the mind itself will be the basis of one's attainment of an enlightened being's body, that is, a buddha's dharmakaya. And in most *Anuttara* Yoga tantras, though not in the Kalachakra, the wind that is the vehicle of the mind will be the basis of the attainment of the form bodies. The contemplation of the four joys on the generation stage is actually a simulation of the genuinely transformative experience of them that will occur on the completion stage. One does not, on the generation stage, actually uproot defilements or directly cognize emptiness; one does, however, lay a powerful basis for those attainments.

The practice of the Yoga of the Drops and the Subtle Yoga concludes with the recitation of mantras that reinforce one's confidence in one's adamantine nature.

The main part of the sadhana completed, one undertakes the "follow-up" practices. These are the recitation of mantras, making offerings and praises, tasting nectar, absorbing the mandala deities, and learning to integrate the practices into everyday life.

Prior to the repetition of mantras, the appropriate seed syllable appears at the heart of each deity. The mantra to be repeated circles the seed syllable, and emanates the host of mandala deities, who first go forth to effect the welfare of sentient beings, and then return to the seed syllable at the deity's heart. The mantra rosaries are reduced to emptiness, then regenerated. Each seed-syllable at each deity's heart emits light rays, which draw down into the mantra-rosary the gnosis and physical attributes of all the tathagatas. As much as possible, then, one recites the mantras of the deities of the mandala, beginning with the *oM ah huM ho haMkshamalavaraya huM phat* of Kalachakra, and continuing through the other mantras of Kalachakra, the mantra of Vishvamata, and then those of the eight shaktis, the male and female tathagatas, the male and female bodhisattvas, the male and female wrathful protectors, and various deities from the speech and body mandalas.

When the repetition of mantras has been completed, one visualizes goddesses, emanated from one's heart, offering to Kalachakra and his entire retinue mouth-water, foot-water, sprinkling water, sipping water, flowers, incense, light, perfume, food, and music. One then makes individual inner offerings to virtually every deity in the mandala, employing the formula *oM*—name of deity—*namah*. Finally, one recites verses praising the attributes of Kalachakra and Vishvamata.

The final act of the meditative session is the absorption of the mandala deities. The circle of great bliss, that is, Kalachakra and Vishvamata, melts into a five-pointed vajra at one's crown, the shaktis melt into a nine-pointed vajra at one's heart, the male and female tathagatas melt into a seventeen pointed vajra at one's forehead, the male and female bodhisattvas and wrathful protectors of the mind mandala melt into a thirty-three pointed vajra at one's throat, the speech yoginis melt into a sixty-five pointed vajra at one's navel, the protectors of the body mandala melt into a thirty-three pointed vajra at one's secret place, the twelve great gods of Hinduism melt into vajras at one's organs of activity, and the nagas and other elementals melt into vajras at one's limbs and fingers. Oneself then melts into emptiness and is regenerated as the simple, one-faced, two-armed Kalachakra, in which form one must try to see oneself during everyday activities. One concludes by dedicating one's merit to the spiritual welfare of sentient beings, and to the personal goal of being reborn in Shambhala, enjoying contact with the gurus and the Dharma in all one's lifetimes, and, through the practice of *Anuttara* Yoga tantra, achieving the supreme level, that of Vajradhara. One may, if one wishes, follow the sadhana with a *torma* offering, either to the protectors or to the dakinis.

Finally, there are instructions for integrating one's sadhana practice into everyday activities. The "yoga of eating" involves reciting certain mantras and prayers to consecrate one's food and drink and offer them up as one would a *torma*. The "yoga of sleeping" involves setting particular syllables that correspond to the tathagata lineages at one's chakras before sleep and attempting to be conscious of the instant of clear light that is a bridge between waking and sleep. The "yoga of rising" involves imagining, upon awakening, that one is being summoned by the drums of dakinis, or the songs of goddesses, and that one arises from clear light in the form of Kalachakra.

During one's daily life, one is instructed to view all activities and processes as the pure sport of blissful gnosis, with all beings as deities, all sounds as mantras, and all places as mandalas. One is instructed, also, that having completed the practices of the generation stage, to progress to the completion stage, whose practices actually will transform one into a fully enlightened buddha, in the form of Kalachakra.

PARTIAL ICONOGRAPHY OF
KALACHAKRA AND VISHVAMATA

		Right		Left
Kalachakra				
			yellow	
Heads		red		white
			black	
Torso			blue	
Arms	white	battle-axe		heads of Brahma
		rod		vajra-chain
		spear		mirror
		discus		conch
	red	hammer		white lotus
		hand-drum		jewel
		vajra-goad		vajra-noose
		fire-arrow		bow
	black	chopper		skull-cup
		trident		katvanga
		sword		shield
		vajra		bell
Legs		red		white
Vishvamata				
			blue	
Heads		white		red
			yellow	
Torso			yellow	
Arms	(yellow)	rosary		jewel
		hand-drum		lotus
		vajra-goad		vajra-noose
		chopper		skull-cup
Legs		yellow		yellow

REFERENCES

My main source for this account is mKhas grub dge legs bzang po's bCom ldan 'das dpal dus kyi 'khor lo'i sku gsung thugs yongs su rdzogs pa'i dkyil 'khor gyi grub thabs *mKhas grub zhal lung zhe bya*, (woodblock print, n.p., n.d., in the collection of Deer Park, Madison, Wisconsin).

I was aided in my research by part of an unpublished translation of the sadhana made by Professor Robert Thurman, and by notes on oral instructions on the Kalachakra sadhana given by the late Khyabje Serkhong Rinpoche at Deer Park in July, 1982. The only Kalachakra sadhana publicly available in English is that in *Kalachakra Initiation: Madison, 1981.* This sadhana was composed by H.H. the Dalai Lama to serve as a six-session yoga practice devoted to Kalachakra.

Further details on the Kalachakra mandala are available in Benoytosh Bhattacharyya, *Nishpannayogavali* Gaekwad's Oriental Series, no.109 (Baroda: Oriental Institute, 1949). Further details on Kalachakra's iconography are found in Bhattacharyya's *Sadhanamala*, Gaekwad's Oriental Series, no.41 (Baroda: Oriental Institute, 1928); and in his *Indian Buddhist Iconography* (London: Oxford University Press, 1924); and Marie-Therése de Mallmann, *Introduction á l'Iconographie du Tântrisme Bouddhique* (Paris: Adrien-Maisonneuve, 1975).

Good general discussions of sadhana may be found in Stephan Beyer's *The Cult of Tara* (Berkeley: University of California Press, 1973), and Giuseppe Tucci, *Theory and Practice of the Mandala* (New York: Samuel Weiser, 1969). Examples of sadhanas may be found in Janice Dean Willis' *The Diamond Light: An Introduction to Tibetan Buddhist Meditations* (New York: Simon & Schuster, 1972); John Blofeld, *The Tantric Mysticism of Tibet* (New York: Dutton, 1970); and Stephan Beyer, *The Buddhist Experience: Sources and Interpretations* Belmont, CA: Dickenson, 1974.

The Subtle Body in Tantric Buddhism[1]

GESHE LHUNDUB SOPA

There are two main schemes for classifying the tantras, a nine-fold and a fourfold scheme.[2] We are following the fourfold scheme, In it, the highest, or *Anuttara*,[3] class is further subdivided into "father" and "mother" tantra according to whether the tantric method (*upaya*) or the tantric wisdom (prajna) predominates in the tantra's practice.[4] The phrase "tantric method" refers to an illusory body. The phrase "tantric wisdom" refers to the knowledge of emptiness inseparable from bliss. The Kalachakra tantra then, is a tantra of the *Anuttara* class, and is usually considered to be a mother tantra.[5]

However, among tantras of the *Anuttara* class, whether father or mother, the Kalachakra has several unique features which are not common to the other tantras. Among these features, the most preeminent is the empty form method of the Kalachakra, in contradistinction to the illusory body method of the other *Anuttara* tantras, like the Guhyasamaja. This brings us to the main subject of our paper, the idea of subtle body, which, in turn, brings us to the traditional idea of the superiority of the tantric method.

When one speaks of the superiority of the tantric method, one is following in the mainstream of later Indian Buddhism and the form in which Buddhism entered and was preserved in Tibet by such illustrious acharyas as Shantarakshita, Padmasambhava,[6] Sa skya Pandita, Atisha,[7] Tsong kha pa, and others too numerous to mention. By "superiority" is meant the advantages which the tantras themselves claim for the tantric method over the other path options offered by Buddhism. In particular, because the tantras are a teaching of the Mahayana, or Great Vehicle, they supplement the "common[8] path" of the Mahayana; "common" here means the Paramitayana, or Perfection Vehicle, which is the path laid out in the Mahayana sutras. Tantra supplements the Perfection Vehicle by the addition of a particular tantric method and wisdom. This is to say that the tantric method is usually held to be in addition to, rather than in place of many of the common paths of the Mahayana sutras.

In the literature of the subject, the perfection or sutra paths are referred to as the vehicle of the cause, or causal vehicle,[9]; the tantric paths are referred to as the vehicle of the effect, or fruition vehicle.[10] It is repeatedly said that the cultivation of the causal vehicle precedes somewhat the attainment of the fruition vehicle. In other words, the development of the Perfection Vehicle goes before the Tantra Vehicle, inasmuch as the former is the very matrix into which the special practices of the Tantra Vehicle should be assimilated.

Here the words "cause" and "effect" refer simply to meditation on the *causes* of enlightenment, in contradistinction to meditation on the final result or effect—enlightenment itself—from the point of view of its qualities and realizations. Thus, the sutra paths teach mainly the cultivation of the causes of enlightenment; these are the virtues of the six (and ten) perfecteds (paramitas). The first four— charity (*dana*), permissible conduct (*shila*), tolerance (*kshanti*), and meditation (dhyana)—count as method (*upaya*), while wisdom (prajna) counts as wisdom (prajna),[11]; strong effort (*virya*) is common to the development of both wisdom and method.[12] These six staples of a bodhisattva's conduct are the causes of enlightenment according to the sutras. The practice of the method side, or the first four perfecteds, is said to produce the corporeal aggregate, or *rupakaya*, of a buddha. The wisdom side is said to produce the realization aggregate, or dharmakaya,[13] of a buddha at the time of achieving perfect enlightenment.

However, from the tantric point of view, the sutras do not reveal fully the causes of the form body of a buddha. Although the virtues of those perfecteds that constitute method may be the *remote* cause of a buddha's form aggregate, the *proximate* cause of this form aggregate is a subtle body which needs to be first generated and subsequently ripened by practices above and beyond the six (or ten) paramitas.

Thus, according to the tantras, the sutra method alone cannot lead beyond the ten bodhisattva stages,[14] and the bodhisattva who has obtained the tenth stage will still have to practice the tantric method in order to progress from the tenth stage to perfect enlightenment[15]. Enlightenment is to be understood as the fulfill-ment not of a single but of a twofold objective: the assured well being of oneself and of others achieved through the attainment, respectively, of the realization body and the form body[16] of a buddha. Specifically, from the meditator's point of view, although the generation of a subtle body is the proximate cause of the form aggregate of perfect enlightenment, the direct or immediate object of its cultivation is the welfare of others.

Finally, according to the tantras, the wisdom achieved by the perfection path alone is excelled by that realized through the tan-tric method. Here, the excellence of wisdom is not being measured in terms of the object realized; that object, emptiness, or shunyata, is the same for both vehicles.. Rather, tantric method excels that of perfection path in terms of the qualities of the realizing mind or mental state; this is a particularly subtle and blissful consciousness often referred to as the "clear light," or *prabhasvara*.

The actual (*don gyi*) clear light is uniquely the product of yoga. This clear light is the realizer of emptiness and simultane-ously an experiencer of great bliss,[17] unlike the neutral conscious-ness realizing emptiness at the culmination of the perfection paths, and therein lies the reason for the tantras claim of bringing about a "superior" wisdom. This realization of emptiness insepara-ble from an experience of great bliss is often called *mahamudra* or "great seal."

Although the actual clear light is solely the product of yoga, it has its analog in ordinary life in another extremely subtle con-sciousness; the tantras hold this, "the clear light of death," together with its supporting material element, to have a close relation with

the vital or biotic force itself.[18] It is named "the clear light of death,"
as an analogy with the "clear light" itself, as this former consciousness is ordinarily dormant, or latent, or potential, appearing as
something only at the time of death. The tantric method seeks by
its yoga practices to arouse this clear light of death, and once it is
manifest, to transform it into a knower of emptiness and so to
produce the actual clear light.

Thus, the tantras profess not only to complete the paths of the
sutras by providing them with an adequate material cause, but also,
by the same methods, to expedite the attainment of the final goal of
the Mahayana. As the vehicle of the fruition, the tantric method of
cultivation does not *per se* focus on the slow, patient accumulation
of virtuous causes, but, rather, focuses directly on the final result,
the form and realization aggregates, by emulating them, in the here
and now, after the fashion of a simulated[19] performance, or a dress
rehearsal. By so meditating, continuously, it seeks to move more
rapidly from mere simulation to the actual reality of its accomplishment. Thus, what is first *pretended* for the purpose of its being
later obtained is divine mind body, and the method of its attainment is the deity yoga of the *Anuttara* tantras, with their two sets
of steps or stages: the steps of generation and the steps of
completion.[20]

The path system of the *Anuttara* tantras might profitably be
called a Buddhist path of apotheosis,[21] of which the *Anuttara* tantras
offer two main types. The Guhyasamaja and its cognate tantras, like
Yamantaka, Chakrasamvara, Vajrayogini etc., represent one such
type, and the Kalachakra the other.

In the path of apotheosis of the Guhyasamaja type, the basis to
be purified is threefold: death, the intermediate state (*anantarabhava*), and birth. The path for doing so is the development of the
union of the illusory body (*maya deha*) and clear light (*prabhasvara*).
The final result is the three pure aggregates (trikaya)[22]: the aggregate of realization (dharmakaya), the aggregate of enjoyment (sambhogakaya), and the aggregate of magical appearance (nirmanakaya); these are also known as the realization body, enjoyment body,
and docetic[23] body respectively. In this sense, death is said to be
purified by the attainment of the realization body, the intermediate
state by the attainment of the enjoyment body, and birth by the
attainment of the docetic body. The means of transition from

death, the intermediate state, and birth to the respective three pure aggregates is the path of cultivating the union of the illusory body and the actual[24] clear light.

The preceding is in the overall or general sense, but in a more specific sense, death may be said to be purified as the actual clear light replaces the ordinary clear light of death. This means that the process together with the subtle mechanism of ordinary death and dying serves as the ground for the deepest realization of emptiness. In the process of ordinary death and dying, the kind of subtle body known as the intermediate-state (or *bardo*) body arises from the pneumatic element of the clear light of death; the intermediate state becomes eventually purified when, in place of the subtle *bardo* body, an illusory body is produced from the material substance of the actual clear light. The phrase "eventually purified" is used because the illusory body first generated from an exemplary clear light[25] is initially impure, later purified, and at length perfected as a buddha's enjoyment body. Finally, birth is said to be purified when, instead of the emergence of the gross body that is ordinarily brought about by the power of karma and *klesha*, there are the special appearances of a body produced for the sake of others; this body results from the perfected union of the pure illusory body with that immediate knowledge of emptiness inseparable from great bliss which constitutes the mind/body of an enlightened buddha.

Thus, in the sequence of path stages (*sa lam*)[26] of cultivation of the Guhyasamaja, the steps of generation mainly ripen the meditator for the practice of the steps of completion. The former anticipate[27] through the use of symbolism and imagination, and they correspond roughly to the first, or path of preparation (*sambhara marga*) subdivision in the fivefold path division[28] of the Perfection Vehicle.

They commence with the meditator's imagining arising from emptiness, passing through a set of transformations, and being generated as the deity[29] together with the deity's mandala (symbolic of the deity's abode) and circle of attendant gods. Here the deity *ishtadevata*, mandala, and entourage of gods represent the nirmanakaya. The steps of generation are said to be concluded when the meditator can visualize lucidly, in every detail, and for as long as desired, the deity, mandala, and circle of gods altogether in a space the size of a mustard seed.

From here begin the steps of completion[30] and the *nonimaginary* process of development leading to the abandonment of the passion (*klesha*) and knowledge (*jneya*) obscurations (*avarana*). In the tantras the knowledge obscurations are understood to be the ordinary, everyday appearances of things, and the passion obscurations are understood to be the apprehension of these ordinary appearances as such.

The steps of completion are sometimes grouped into five, sometimes into six steps. When grouped into six, the first three are the three withdrawals or isolations, i.e., of the body, the speech, and the mind, followed by the steps of illusory body, clear light, and union.[31] The three withdrawals of the body, speech, and mind comprise a set of steps recapitulating the stages of dying. Through the first, the pneumatic elements or winds that are the support or vehicle of consciousness are successively withdrawn from their ordinary activities and first made to enter the central channel,[32] or *avadhuti*, then to abide there, and finally to be dissolved there. Through the second, various knots which constrict the movement of wind through the central channel are loosened sufficiently to permit the winds to enter, abide, and be dissolved in the heart area of the central channel. By the third, the final knots are loosened, and the winds are made to enter, abide, and be dissolved into a point, little larger than a mustard seed, in the heart region, which is the seat of the vital force itself. The dissolution of all the pneumatic elements into this "indestructable drop"[33] completes the recapitulation of the act of dying, and there arises a manifestation of the clear light, called the "exemplary clear light."[34]

This exemplary clear light, having been produced by yoga, is more refined than the ordinary clear light of death, but is not yet the actual clear light. This corresponds roughly to the path of reaching (*prayoga marga*) of the fivefold path system, wherein an approximate but not a final direct understanding of emptiness is achieved. Here, the clear light of death includes no understanding of emptiness, whereas the *exemplary* clear light closely approaches but does not quite reach the final direct knowing of emptiness. The production of this exemplary clear light marks the climax of the three withdrawals and serves as the material cause for the cultivation of the next step, the production of the impure illusory body.

To summarize very briefly the remaining steps: before the stage of union, the clear light and illusory body exist alternately, and not at the same time. Then, at the stage of union, the meditator utilizes the impure illusory body as a basis for bringing about a new manifestation of the clear light; this time, it is the actual clear light which directly perceives emptiness. This production corresponds to the Perfection Vehicle's path of seeing (*darshana marga*), on which those obscurations which can be abandoned by seeing reality directly are abandoned. Here, on the tantric path, all the remaining obscurations are relinquished through the final steps of the path, and again, these correspond to the Perfection Vehicle's path of cultivation (*bhavana marga*), on which the most subtle knowledge obscurations are abandoned.

On the tantric path, this is accomplished through still another production of illusory body, this time the pure illusory body which stays conjoined with the actual clear light. This conjunction is the union (*yuganaddha*) of clear light and illusory body. Through the utilization of this union, the final stages of purification of the obscurations are accomplished, and these in turn are climaxed by a path of no more training (*ashaiksha marga*). This "path" is the realization of enlightenment itself through the attainment of the three bodies.

The above has been a highly abbreviated sketch of the sequence of path stages of the Guhyasamaja, with minimal elaboration and without discussion of the various meditation techniques utilized in the development of a path of this sort, as each of these topics is large in itself and all together quite voluminous, and this is to say nothing of the many specific philosophical, scientific, etc., types of problems which a subject matter of this sort will pose for this or that particular reader.

In general, the *Anuttara* tantras (with some exceptions on the side of the Kalachakra) teach the development of a path system of the above kind. Some, like Yamantaka, etc., give a greater emphasis and expatiation to the generation and development of illusory body; others, like the Chakrasamvara, Vajrayogini, etc., give emphasis to the generation and development of clear light. Furthermore, there are a great many specific differences in the details of the forms of the *yidam* to be visualized, the particulars of the mandalas,

and numerous other such characteristics. However, the fundamental basis of purification (i.e., death, intermediate state, and birth),
the path (i.e., the cultivation of the union of illusory body and clear
light), and the final result (i.e., the three bodies), remain a constant
in the many *anuttara* tantras (excepting the Kalachakra).

Still another important feature shared by all of the above (again
excepting the Kalachakra) is the teaching that enlightenment is
often achieved not in the current life but in the intermediate state.
Therfore, without passing straight on to the Kalachakra, the writer
would like to digress for a moment to the subject of the attainment
of the final goal in the intermediate state (*antarabhava; bardo*).

The notion of an intermediate state and its subtle *bardo* body is
not peculiar to the tantras, but is common to all of Buddhhism;[35]
these are found in both the Hinayana and Mahayana sutras and
their commentaries. Principal commentarial sources for the
Hinayana may be found in Book III of Vasubandhu's *Abhidharma-
kosa*, and like sources for the Mahayana are Asanga's *Abhidharmasamuccaya* and the *Bhumivastu* section of his *Yogacaryabhumi*.

Similarly, the teaching that many who are proceeding on the
path achieve the final goal in the *bardo* is shared as well by the
Hinayana and the common Mahayana. For instance, Vasubandhu
says in Book VI of the *Kosa*, "non-returners, by the exhaustion of
these nine, are (obtainers of) nirvana in the intermediate (state, or
the next) life, (and then) with difficulty, or without difficulty."[36]
These two lines occur in a longer passage discussing twenty
Sanghas[37] (i.e., twenty kinds of aryan individuals proceeding on the
aryan paths[38]). The twenty is from the point of view of two subdivisions (i.e., entry and abiding) in the four fruitions (i.e., stream
winner, once returner, non-returner, and arahant), making eight,
together with variable subdivisions within this resultant eight.
These two lines state that some who have become non-returners
because of having exhausted nine *kleshas* (passions) belonging to
the desire realm achieve arahantship (1) either in the intermediate
state or (2) in the next life, and if the latter, either (3) with difficulty,
or (4) easily in that next life. The longer passage continues that
those who do not realize nirvana by one of the above four proceed
to yet another birth, but in a higher region of the form realm.
Likewise, in Book I of the *Abhisamayalamkara*, touching on the topic
of the same twenty Sanghas, it says, in similar language, "In the

intermediate (state, or the next) life, hard, (or) easily...."[39] The
Abhisamayakamkara, being a Mahayana work and a commentary on
the *Prajnaparamita* sutras, is referring the twenty Sanghas analogi-
cally to the paths of Bodhisattvas also. Thus, for both the Hinayana
and the common Mahayana, one of the modes of achieving the
final goal is in the intermediate state, just as it is for the uncommon, or tantric, Mahayana.

There is, however, this difference, that for the Hinayana and
common Mahayana, the one attaining the final goal in the intermediate state possesses a *bardo* body at the time of attainment, whereas
for the tantric Mahayana, such an attainer no longer is experienc-
ing a *bardo* body, since such a body has already given way to an
illusory body, and it is through the illusory body that the final goal
is attained by the adept in tantra, whether in the *bardo* or in life.

One of the features of the method of the Kalachakra that
sharply distinguishes it from the other *Anuttara* tantras is the
absence of *bardo* as one of the bases of purification. With the
absence of *bardo*, there is an absence of illusory body in the above
sense as well. Notwithstanding, the Kalachakra does develop
another kind of subtle body (*shukshma deha*), usually referred to as
"empty form" (*stong gzugs*). Consequently, in the Kalachakra the
"immediate realization of emptiness inseparable from bliss" is
held to have a sense slightly different from its meaning in the other
anuttara tantras.[40] In the Kalachakra, the "empty" in emptiness
refers to empty form, and "bliss" to the experience of the mind
directly knowing emptiness.[41]

The *Kalachakra Tantra* itself, together with its great commentary,
the *Vimalaprabha*,[42] and subsequent commentarial literature, cover
extensively and in detail a wide ranging subject matter, all of which
may be grouped under three topics: an Outer Kalachakra (or
Wheel of Time), an Inner Kalachakra, and an Other Kalachakra.
The Outer Kalachakra deals with the universe conventionalized[43]
into a system of cosmology, the Inner Kalachakra with the structures, meta-structures and functions of the human body (most
notably the channels, winds, and seminal drops), and the Other
Kalachakra with the path of the generation and completion stages
and its final result.

In the path of the Kalachakra, just as in the path of the Guhyasamaja type, the bases of purification are the same for both the steps

of generation and the steps of completion. Here, however, the Other Kalachakra takes as the bases of purification the outer and inner wheels of time, that is the outer and inner worlds as conventionalized and set forth in the Kalachakra tantras.

Among the various meta-structures of the Inner Kalachakra, four in particular serve as special bases for the path. These are four seminal drops or germs which are identified as the "germs of the four kinds of states," and are located in the head, throat, heart, and navel regions of the central channel. Together, they are said to be the roots of all the obscurations.[44] Hence, by purifying these, all the obscurations can be removed.

The four states, of which these are the seed, are four states of consciousness, namely the waking state, the dreaming state, the deep sleep state, and the fourth state. In ordinary life, the first state produces the appearances of the various objects of the five senses and of the mental consciousness. The second state produces syllables, terms, and language, etc. The third produces a diffuse and vague awareness. The fourth produces orgasm. When completely purified, they result in four vajras[45] (or four sovereigns): vajra-body, vajra-speech, vajra-mind, and vajra-bliss. As the path of purification, the first is the empty forms that will ripen as vajra-body, the second, the subtle mantric sounds that will ripen as vajra-speech, the third, the nondiscursive wisdom of realization that will ripen as vajra-mind, and the fourth, the wisdom of great bliss that will ripen as vajra-bliss. These four vajras may also be understood as coextensive with the three bodies: vajra-body being equivalent to the nirmanakaya, vajra-speech to the sambhogakaya,[46] and vajra-mind together with vajra-bliss to the dharmakaya.[47]

As for the path of completion, this is coextensive with the famous six-part yoga (*shadangayoga*) of the Kalachakra, a set of six sequential stages. The six are: collection, absorption, wind control, retention, mindfulness, and enrapture.[48] For the purpose of understanding the path, these may be arranged in three pairs, each pair laying the groundwork for the attainment of one of the three bodies. The former of each pair is like an entry into a new phase or process and the latter like its strengthening or confirmation.

Thus, collection/absorption are for realizing the nirmanakaya. Wind control/retention are for realizing the sambhogakaya. Mindfulness/enrapture are for realizing the dharmakaya. Quite briefly, then, collection/absorption gather together the winds and make them manageable for use. Wind control/retention make them enter into the central channel and penetrate the "germs of the four kinds of states." Mindfulness/enrapture bring about union[49] and through union the entry into and accomplishment of the aryan path.

However, most of the salient features of the steps of this path do not require mention in a paper dealing mainly with the subject of subtle body. The Kalachakra is a mother tantra, and consequently its completion stages mainly emphasize the path of integrating emptiness and great bliss. Thus, passing over these many, although important, details, we may hasten to refer to the corporeal side of this path (i.e., the body of empty form).

Although the empty form of the Kalachakra deity is generated at the very beginning of the completion stages[50], it remains little more than an extension of the imaginary form produced from the samadhi sealing the climax of the steps of generation.[51] It is not until the time of the union[52] achieved by the practice of the fifth limb of mindfulness, that this empty form comes into its own, for it is the union achieved by this practice which becomes the proximate cause of the mind/body of perfect enlightenment.

When this union is achieved, the entire remaining path may be quite rapidly obtained by the sixth or final part, the limb of enrapture.[53] Through it all, the winds which are the support of samsaric consciousness are stopped. According to the Kalachakra there are 21,600 such karmic winds which course through the body in a daily circuit. All these winds are to be withdrawn and the circuit stopped. With the cessation of this daily circuit, samsaric consciousness likewise ceases. Here, the chief method of realizing this cessation is through the cultivation of a sufficiently powerful antidote. Such an antidote is the yogic realization of emptiness inseparable from unchanging bliss. The production and fortification of such a realization is the function of the final limb or part of the six-part yoga, called "enrapture."

Within this final part, the main procedure for effecting this might be translated as "piling up" (brtsegs pa). Here, the reader must backtrack for a moment. Through collection and absorption, the winds are made more and more manageable. Then, through wind control they are made to enter the central channel. Then, due to their retention in the central channel, a subtle psychic heat (*gtum mo*) is generated in the lower region. Then, the union achieved through mindfulness intensifies the psychic heat, making it blaze upward through the central channel, causing the *bodhicitta* (or white *thig le*)[54] in the head region of the central channel to melt. Finally, through enrapture, the molten seminal drops of the white *bodhicitta* begin to pile up or become stacked from the bottom[55] of the central channel, and with each increase a higher and higher level of yogic realization is attained; with these attainments there is a cutting off of an increasing number of karmic winds.[56] Thereby, the aryan path is entered upon and completed.

In this final part of the six-part yoga, the path is divided into twelve. The first section corresponds to the path of preparation; the second corresponds to the first of the ten levels (*dashabhumi*) and is coextensive with the path of seeing; the third through the eleventh to the path of cultivation and is coextensive with the second through the tenth of the ten levels; and finally, the twelfth corresponds to the path of no further training, or enlightenment itself.

Thus, with the accumulation of the white and red *bodhicitta* in each of the twelve regions of the central channel, the necessary yogic realization is generated to bring about a rapid traversal of the path to the final goal: the attainment of the three perfect bodies of final enlightenment.

Here, the Kalachakra teaches that with each piling up of the *bodhicitta*, the gross physical body is progressively consumed leaving in the end the pure body of the Kalachakra deity of empty form, like the elixir which dissolves iron, transforming it into pure gold. With the disappearance of the gross body, the piled up *bodhicitta* vanishes as well. Thus, the Kalachakra path becomes in the end like a kind of alchemy.

With this, we are brought back to the topic with which we began this discussion, that the Kalachakra does not utilize the *bardo* as a basis of purification. Because of the relations between the gross and subtle bodies in the Kalachakra, the subtle body of the *bardo*, or "illusory" type, cannot support the development of the Kalachakra path. Only the gross physical body is provided with the meta-structuring necessary to do this. This difference, and others such as we have noted above, have given rise to a great deal of discussion, and sometimes controversy, within native Tibetan scholarship. Such discussions[57] are beyond the scope of this paper.

We conclude by noting that the Kalachakra path does not particularly lend itself to such brief treatment. As explained earlier, the Kalachakra path takes as its basis of purification the multifarious conventions of the outer and inner Kalachakra, i.e., its intricate systems of cosmology and meta-physiology. Notwithstanding these difficulties, we have tried somewhat to delineate the Kalachakra path against the background of the other *Anuttara* tantras, especially with respect to its treatment of subtle body.

NOTES

1. This paper had its origin as a rather long footnote to a larger paper, "Some Notes Contextualizing the Kalachakra," which was prepared for delivery at the sixth IABS Conference in Tokyo, Japan, in September of 1983. I would like to thank Elvin W. Jones for his editorial and literary assistance in the preparation of this paper.

2. According to the ninefold classification: three Sutrayana, i.e., Shravaka, Pratyekabuddha, and Bodhisattva; three outer Mantrayana, i.e., *Kriya, Charya* and Yoga; and three inner unsurpassable, i.e., *Mahayoga, Anuyoga* and *Atiyoga*. Vid. Nyingma section, page 7 of Thu'u khan chos kyi nyi ma's *History of the Tibetan Sects, Legs bshad shel gyi me long.*

    According to the fourfold classification: *Kriya, Charya,* Yoga, and *Anuttara; Kriya* emphasizes mainly outer action, *Charya* half outer-half inner action, Yoga inner action, *Anuttara* highest inner action.

3. *anuttara = anuttarayoga*

4. In addition to the subdivision of father and mother tantra, *anuttara* tantras are often classified as nondual. Here, however, "nondual" does not refer to the nonduality of method and wisdom, but to the nonduality of emptiness and bliss. In this sense, all *anuttara* tantras are nondual. However, a great deal of discussion on such points has arisen on account of such terms and expressions, which are to be found in the tantras themselves.

5. The Kalachakra tantra is frequently also called a nondual tantra. For the sense of this, see note 4 above.

6. Tucci's speculation in *Minor Buddhist Texts* that history has perhaps overestimated the concord between the followers of Shantarakshita and Padmasambhava may be gratuitous. While pointing to no evidence in particular it ignores the fact that Shantarakshita, aside from being the great systematizer of the *Yoga-charasvatantrika-Madhyamika*, is often counted as one of the principal acharyas of *Kriya* tantra.

7. By the time of Atisha's coming to Tibet in the eleventh century, Buddhism in Tibet had become badly fragmented, due to gLang dar ma's persecution of Buddhism and the disruption following his assassination and the breakdown of the old kingship. Some, for example, following the Vinaya, despised the tantras, and many following the tantras ignored and neglected the Vinaya, etc. Consequently, a large part of Atisha's work in Tibet was the reintegration of Buddhism. In this work of reintegration, Atisha taught the superiority of the tantras, and in this he was followed later by Tsong kha pa.

8. The Mahayana, being both the vehicle of the sutras (Sutrayana = Paramita-yana) and the vehicle of the tantras (Tantrayana = Mantrayana), the common path means the path common to or shared by both systems of the Mahayana, for many principal elements of the Mahayana *qua* Mahayana are taught mainly in the sutras rather than in the tantras, elements like details of the

bodhisattva vows, the practice of the paramitas, many of the salient features of understanding emptiness, or of the development of *bodhicitta*, etc. Such features represent the common path, i.e., common to the perfection and tantric paths.

9.   *rgyu'i theg pa*

10. *bras bu'i theg pa*

11. "Wisdom (prajna) as wisdom (prajna)," i.e., wisdom, or prajnaparamita, which constitutes one of the six perfecteds, as the wisdom which is one of the contrasting pair of wisdom and method (prajna and *upaya*).

12. Meditation (samadhi) is sometimes counted together with wisdom (prajna) on the wisdom side.

13. Body (kaya) does not mean "corporeity" but, rather, "an aggregate of qualities." Consequently, as we are not translating, we will often refer to "kaya" by way of its paraphrase as "aggregate."

14. *Sa bchu (dashabhumi).*

15. i.e., Buddhahood itself, the level immediately following the ten stages and the fulfillment of the entire Mahayana path.

16. In the Mahayana, the form body (*rupakaya*) may be subdivided into a sambhogakaya and a nirmanakaya, the former is a buddha's natural or own form (*svarupakaya*), and the latter is any number of corporeal manifestations presented by a buddha to others for the purposes of leading or instructing them. Other than to the buddhas themselves, the sambhogakaya is said to be visible only to bodhisattvas of the ten stages.

17. When one speaks of a realization of emptiness inseparable from great bliss, one is referring to a *cognitum*-cognizer (*vishaya-vishayin*) relation. This is to say that emptiness itself is the direct object, or *cognitum*, of a mind cognizing it, whereas bliss is a mental quality belonging to the cognizing mind itself.

18. This biotic force is envisaged as the subtlest pneumatic element, which is inseparable from the subtlest consciousness. According to the tantras, there is no moment of consciousness or mind which is not associated with some sort of corporeal element that serves as its vehicle. Thus, the tantras will not admit to a realm of disembodied consciousness such as the Hinayana holds the formless realm (*arupaloka*), with its four subdivisions, to be. Even here, the tantras maintain the existence of a kind of subtle form, for wherever there is mind, they say there is also a corporeity on which, in a manner of speaking, it may be said to ride. These mounts of the mind are held to be the pneumatic element or winds (*gzhon pa'i rlung*) of the other elements. Of these winds, the most subtle is the life force itself (*srog rlung = gnyug ma'i rlung*), the vehicle of the most subtle consciousness (*gnyug ma'i sems*). During life, this pair of subtlest wind and consciousness are said to reside together in a point often called the "indestructible drop" (*mi shigs pa'i thig le*) which persists through the course of an entire life in the area of the heart. The consciousness associated

with this pair becomes apparent in death itself as a vacuous, contentless lucidity, i.e., the clear light of death. Subsequently, the material side of this pair serves as a seed for the generation of a subtle body form in the intermediate state, a form called the "intermediate state body" (*bar do'i lus*). Similarly, it is the same subtle wind which provides the base for the production of an illusory body (*rgyu ma'i lus*) through the cultivation of *anuttara* yoga.

For further details concerning the ideas of death and dying to be found in the *anuttara* tantras see *Death, Intermediate State and Rebirth in Tibetan Buddhism*, by Lati Rinbochay and Jeffrey Hopkins, London: Rider and Company, 1979.

19. Development of superior qualities and behavior through a mode of esoteric imitation or simulation (*rnam pa mthun par*) is one of the salient features of tantric yoga.

20. *utpattikrama* and *sampannakrama*

21. i.e., apotheosis in its simple literal sense of transformation or metamorphosis from a human into a divine being.

22. Re: three pure aggregates (trikaya), see notes 13 and 16 above.

23. In contradistinction to a buddha's sambhogakaya, i.e., a buddha's actual or own body that is apprehended by a buddha, the apparitional or docetic body (nirmanakaya) is a buddha's heuristic projection of a seeming or appearance of body to another. Thus, by a kind of Mahayana docetism, Shakyamuni, the historical founder of Buddhism, is just one such nirmanakaya, albeit a very special one called *paramanirmanakaya*, the most excellent docetic body.

24. In the body of this paper, three things are being designated as "clear light" and are distinguished as: clear light of death (*'chi ba'i 'od gsal*), exemplary clear light (*dpe'i 'od gsal*), and actual clear light (*don gyi 'od gsal*).

25. For explanation of this exemplary clear light, see page 53 in text.

26. There are numerous commentaries on the path stages of the Guhyasamaja. Here, we are following mainly *gSang chen rgyud sde bzhi'i sa lam gyi rnam gzhag rgyud gzhung gsal byed*, by Ngag dbang dpal ldan, and *dP'al gsang ba 'dus pa 'phags lugs dang mthun pa'i sngags kyi sa lam rnam gzhag legs bshad skal bzang 'jug ngogs*, by dByangs can dga' ba'i blo gros.

27. They anticipate inasmuch as the bases of purification, i.e., death, the intermediate, and birth, are the same for both the stages of generation and of completion, the former being mainly imaginary and the latter actual.

28. fivefold subdivision of the path (= fivefold path) of the Paramitayana, i.e., *sambhara marga, prayoga marga, darshana marga, bhavana marga*, and *ashaikya marga*, respectively the preparatory path, path of reaching, path of seeing, path of cultivation, path of no further training. Here, the path of seeing is coextensive with the first of the ten stages, and the path of cultivation with the remaining nine of the ten stages, and the path of no further training with enlightenment itself.

29. Deity = the *yidam* (*ishtadevata*). The *anuttara* tantras center on various such deities, and here in the *Guhyasamaja*, the deity, of course, is Guhyasamaja himself.

30. Here, in his *Sa lam* (op. cit.) dByangs can dga' ba'i blo gros characterizes the steps of completion as completing because they are steps of meditation which do not have recourse to the imagination but rather target actual *loci* of the human body, the channels, wind, and drops. *"Blos btags pa la ma ltos par rang grub tsam nas rdzogs pa'i lus kyi rtsa rlung thig le la gnad du bsnun nas bsgom par bya ba'i rim pa yin pas de ltar brjod pa'i phyir."*

31. When classified into five steps, the first two steps, i.e., body and speech, of the sixfold classification are subsumed by a single withdrawal of speech, the following four, withdrawal of mind to union, remaining the same. The five-fold classification is particularly venerable as based on the system of Nagarjuna.

32. In the metaphysiology of the tantras, there are three principal elements which are objects of the meditation that aims at effecting the psychophysical developments achieved on the tantric paths. These are the channels or veins (*rtsa*), wind or pneumatic element (*rlung*), and seminal drops or germ (*thig le*). These three elements for the most part occupy a level of subtlety intermediate between the gross body of flesh and bone and the finest corporeal essence represented by the "indestructible germ" which the tantras hold to be the root of samsara and nirvana. Of these, the veins form a quasianatomical network of seventy-two thousand channels through which course the winds. This ramous structure branches off from a relatively few chief ramiform channels, the principal of which are the medial channel and two channels to the right and left of it, respectively *rkyang ma* and *ro ma*, these three along with two others being the first to form in the ontogeny of the individual. These three intertwine in numerous places, thereby creating strictures or knots which ordinarily prevent the movement of the winds through the medial channel, whereas juncture points of other channels create various *nexi* often called "wheels" or "chakra," which are of considerable importance in the process of yoga. In ordinary life, the winds do not deeply penetrate and abide in the medial channel except through the action of death, and thus the deep penetration of this channel and the loosening of the knots is one of the principal jobs of the initial stages of the steps of completion. The winds have been briefly discussed above in note 18, but while they have numerous other functions in growth, bodily processes, etc., we have been able to mention only their importance for the tantras as vehicles of consciousness. Finally, the third of the above elements, the drops or germ (*thig le*) are seminal somatic essences both male and female, respectively white and red, which eventuate in multiform structures like flesh, blood, bone, etc.

    Additional information may be found in *Death, Intermediate State, and Rebirth in Tibetan Buddhism* (op. cit.).

33. "Indestructible germ" or "drop" has two referents, i.e., the inseparable union of the subtlest mind/wind like kernel, and the red and white *thig le*, which, like

the husk, encloses them in the region of the heart, the latter *thig le* being indestructible only during the duration of a present lifetime.

34. i.e., *dpe'i 'od gsal*. See note 24.

35. i.e., Buddhism as it developed in India and wherever such developments are preserved elsewhere.

36. *de dgu zad bas phyir mi'ong/ de ni bar skyes 'du byed dang/ 'du byed med yongs mya ngan 'da'/*

37. In the Vinaya, a Sangha will ordinarily consist minimally of four fully ordained bhiksus. However, a bhiksu or bhiksuni who has obtained the aryan path and thus become an aryan may perform all the functions of a Sangha in his or her own person. Consequently, here, the twenty Sanghas refer to twenty kinds of aryan individuals.

38. In the fivefold division of the path (See note 28 above) the first two divisions are the path of ordinary individuals (*prithagjana*), whereas the remaining three divisions are the path of the aryans or aryan individual. The point of entry into the aryan path is the first moment of the *darshana marga*, or direct (i.e., nonconceptual, like sense perception) and unerroneous realization of ultimate reality, for only with this kind of realization of truth does every type of purification become attainable.

39. ...*Bar skyes nas dang/ byed dang byed min*...

40. *sku dag pa sgyu ma'i sku dang thugs dag pa bde stong dbyer med kyi ye shes gnyis gzuug du 'jug pa.* = *gzung 'jug gi sku* in Kalachakra.

41. Here a reader should not confuse "empty" in "empty form" and "empty" in "emptiness." The former refers only to a special kind of subtle body, and the latter refers to ultimate reality.

42. The *Vimalaprabha* consists of five books, respectively devoted to elucidation of the topics of: Cosmology, Metaphysiology, Initiation, Sadhana, and Yogic realization (jnana).

43. "Conventionalized into a system of cosmology..." because commentaries dealing with the subject of the Kalachakra, like Bu ston Rinpoche's commentary on the *Vimalaprabha*, often state that its cosmology is not to be taken as of direct meaning (*nitartha; nges don*), i.e., as literally true, but rather that its cosmology represents an accommodation to the views of the persons to who the Buddha taught this particular path to enlightenment. Buddhism in India had two principal systems of cosmology, that of the Abhidharma and that of the Kalachakra, with many differences between them.

44. "Roots of all the obscurations," words which occur in the tantra itself, is actually being said of the potencies of the mind/wind union which each of these seminal drops incorporates. This also a sharp contrast to the concentration of the Guhyasamaja type yoga on the "indestructible drop" which it utilizes as the psychic and material base for transformations into the perfect

mind/body of enlightenment.

45. *Vajra* is sometimes translated as "diamond," that is, the lord of stone which can cut all other substances, and sometimes as "thunderbolt," referring to the scepter of authority of Indra, the king of the gods. In either instance, there is a strong sense of the sovereignty which rules over all others of its kind.

46. Not only for the Kalachakra, but for all the other *Anuttara* Yoga tantras as well, the special or uncommon (that is unshared by the Paramitayana) attainment of the sambhogakaya is its aggregation of vocalizations. For the tantras, the speech element predominates in the sambhogakaya, whereas the form, or corporeal element, predominates in the nirmanakaya.

47. In the tantras, sometimes four bodies are counted. The four bodies are just the three bodies (trikaya) plus a *svabhavakaya (ngo bo nyid sku)*. Here, the *svabhavakaya* represents the cessations *(nirodha)* achieved by a buddha and also the realization of emptiness. As in the tantras, realization of emptiness is inseparable from the experience of great bliss; vajra-bliss assimilates to the *svabhavakaya* in the four kaya system, and to the dharmakaya in the three kaya system.

48. 1. *so sor bsdud pa*, 2. *bsam rtan*, 3. *srog rtsol*, 4. *'dzin pa*, 5. *rjes dran*, and 6. *ting 'dzin*.

49. i.e. union of the Kalachakra deity and his consort, each generated as a body of empty form in the navel area. See note 52.

50. This empty form of the Kalachakra deity is produced from a substance (there is a great deal of controversy on this point) which appears at the climax of a series of withdrawals and dissolutions of the consciousness-supporting winds. In the Kalachakra, the series is tenfold: four appearances associated with the four elements of earth, water, fire, and air, called night appearances; and six associated with particular forms of consciousness, called day appearances. The day appearances are said to be much harder to realize. The four night appearances are smoke, mirage, sparks, and flame of a butter lamp followed by the six day appearances, i.e., sun (like at the end of a great eon), moon, sun *rahula* (eclipse), lightning, and a blue *thig le*. In the center of this blue seminal drop is a speck of black substance in which appears the Kalachakra deity. This substance is taken as a basis for the production of empty form, and from it the body of the Kalachakra deity is generated. This leads us to note similarities and differences to a like series of eight appearances utilized in the Guhya-samaja when the consciousness-supporting winds are withdrawn. This eight-fold series ends in the appearance of the clear light. An effort to elucidate this subject further would require the introduction of several additional topics too large for this small paper.

51. As above, the steps of generation of the Kalachakra are said to end when the meditator can visualize clearly, in every detail, and for as long as the meditator desires, the deity with mandala and entourage of gods in a space the size of a mustard seed. This is a specifically tantric development of the meditative fixation *(shamatha)* which is developed on all the Buddhist paths. The produc-

tion of the form of the Kalachakra deity at the earlier stages is little more than an extension of this imaginative power of visualization.

52. In the initial stages of this union developed during the practice of mindful-ness, there is not yet a direct yogic realization of emptiness. At this time, i.e., during the steps of mindfulness, one generates oneself as the Kalachakra deity with consort as a body of empty form in union in the navel area for the first time. Through this union great bliss is realized. Subsequently, this realiza-tion of great bliss is made also to become a realizer of emptiness. This full realization of emptiness arises later, during the early stages of the practice of enrapture, specifically, with the "piling up" of the first 1800 seminal drops in the central channel, an action which immobilizes an equal number of the 21,600 karmic winds. This also brings about the completion of the path of reaching (*prayoga marga*) and entry into the path of seeing (*darshana marga*), the beginning of the aryan path.

53. One of the features of the *shadangayoga* worth noting is its enormous prepara-tion of a technical yogic kind, extending through all the first five of the six parts, at length to be followed on the sixth by a rapid completion of the entire Mahayana path, beginning from the upper level of the path of preparation (*sambhara marga*) all the way to the attainment of the final goal.

54. The uncommon *bodhicitta* of the tantras are the white and red *thig le*. The white descending and the red ascending meet in the heart just before death. Accord-ingly, death is considered complete when each exits from the body at the opposite ends of the central channel from which it began its movement. These white and red seminal drops are also utilized in tantric yoga for the production of subtle states of consciousness, and as the material cause for subtle kinds of body.

55. With the piling up of the white *bodhicitta* from the bottom of the central channel, there is also an inverse and commensurate piling up of the red *bodhicitta* from the top.

56. For the purposes of this yoga, the central channel must be divided into seven key points and their six interstices and twelve semi-interstices, and the entire 21,600 karmic winds are grouped into twelve sets of 1800. Thus, with the accumulation of 1800 *thig le* in each of these twelve divisions of the central channel (that is in the twelve semi-interstices), a sufficiency of yogic realiza-tion is generated to annihilate a comparable area of karmic winds.

57. Here, for instance, the reader who can read Tibetan might refer to the ques-tions and answers concerning the Kalachakra to be found in *dPal dus kyi 'khor lo i sa lam gyi gnos 'dzin rag rim 'phros dang bcas pa mkhas grub smra ba'i nyi ma'i zhal lung*, by Jam dbyangs dgyes pa'i bshes gnyen.

ERRATA

These articles have been photographically reproduced from the original publication. The following are author corrections to the original.

Page 3, line 25 for "teaching to the Dharma" read "teaching of the Dharma"

Page 11, line 38 for "sacrifice finding that in the final analysis" read "sacrifice the possibility that in the final analysis"

Page 14, line 28 for "the realism and the *apparent* nihilism" read "the realism of the first turning and the *apparent* nihilism"

Page 15, lines 4-5 for "Although religiously," read "Religiously,"

Page 30, lines 1-7 should read "The final procedure, "union" *(yuganaddha),* involves the final elimination of defilements through the joint activities of the actual clear light and purified illusory body, and completes the transformation of one's mind and body into the dharmakaya and sambhogakaya and nirmanakayas of a fully enlightened buddha."

Page 31, line 28 for "topics in any detail" read "topics in such detail"

Page 35, line 1 for "in substance or soteriology" read "in substance and soteriology"

Page 42, line 15 for "of the Conqueror's (children)" read "of the Conqueror's children"

Page 44, Section 3, line 11 for "Vasubadhu" read "Vasubandhu"

Page 47, Section 9, line 2 for "Helmut Goffmann" read "Helmut Hoffmann"

Page 62, line 26 for "Adhibuddha!" read "Adhibuddha!""

Page 93, line 7 for "60,000-verse on the *Mulatantra*" read "60,000-verse commentary on the *Mulatantra*"

Page 97, line 37 for "to determine which of the tathagata lineages" read "to determine with which of the tathagata lineages"

Page 102, line 1 for "THE CROWN *(Cod pa)* INITIATION" read "THE CROWN *(Cod pan)* INITIATION"

Page 117, note 23 for "*The Collected Works of Longdol Lama*... pp.270-275" read "*The Collected Works of Longdol Lama*... vol.1, pp.270-275"

Page 119, line 9 for "accomplishing *sgrub*" read "accomplishing *(sgrub)*"

Page 130, line 29 for "moon-lake drop" read "moon-like drop"

Page 133, line 13 for "and the world are as the play" read "and the world are seen as the play"

Page 134, line 4 for "an enlightened being's body" read "an enlightened being's mentality"

Page 141, lines 24-25 for "tantric method excells that of perfection path" read "tantric method surpasses that of the perfection path"

Page 143, lines 35-36 for "deity *ishtadevata*, mandala, and entourage" read "deity *(ishtadevata)*, mandala, and entourage"

Page 142, lines 29-30 for "intermediate state *(anantarabhava)*" read "intermediate state *(antarabhava)*"

Page 156, note 44, line 3 for "This also a sharp contrast" read "This also is a sharp contrast"